M000236293

Mercies

ANNE SEXTON was born in Newton, Massachusetts, in 1928. Her first mental breakdown with post-partum depression occurred after the birth of her elder daughter in 1953; repeated hospitalizations followed throughout her life. Her therapist encouraged her to write, and in 1957 she joined poetry workshops in Boston which would bring her into the orbit of Maxine Kumin, Robert Lowell and Sylvia Plath. Her books are *To Bedlam and Part Way Back* (1960), *All My Pretty Ones* (1962), the Pulitzer Prize-winning *Live or Die* (1966), *Love Poems* (1969), *Transformations* (1971), *The Book of Folly* (1973), *The Death Notebooks* (1974) and the posthumous volumes *The Awful Rowing Toward God* (1975), *45 Mercy Street* (1976) and *Words for Dr. Y.* (1978). She committed suicide in October 1974 at the age of 45.

Born in 1953 in Newton, Massachusetts, LINDA GRAY SEXTON graduated from Harvard with a degree in literature in 1975. After the death of her mother, Linda became the Literary Executor of the Estate of Anne Sexton, and edited several posthumous books of her mother's poetry. She is the author of a number of works of non-fiction, fiction and memoir, including *Between Two Worlds: Young Women in Crisis* (1979), *Rituals* (1981), *Points of Light* (1988), *Searching for Mercy Street: My Journey Back to My Mother, Anne Sexton* (1994) and *Half in Love: Surviving the Legacy of Suicide* (2011).

ANNE SEXTON

Mercies

Selected Poems

Selected and introduced by Linda Gray Sexton

PENGUIN BOOKS

PENGUIN CLASSICS

UK | USA | Canada | Ireland | Australia
India | New Zealand | South Africa

Penguin Classics is part of the Penguin Random House group of companies
whose addresses can be found at global.penguinrandomhouse.com

This collection published in Penguin Books 2020
003

Poems copyright © The Estate of Anne Sexton, 1960, 1962, 1966, 1969, 1971,
1972, 1974, 1975, 1976, 1978, 1981
Selection and introduction copyright © Linda Gray Sexton, 2020

Set in 10.5/13 pt Dante MT Std
Typeset by Jouve (UK), Milton Keynes
Printed and bound in Great Britain by Clays Ltd, Elcograf S.p.A.

A CIP catalogue record for this book is available from the British Library

ISBN: 978-0-241-46039-9

www.greenpenguin.co.uk

MIX
Paper from
responsible sources
FSC® C018179

Penguin Random House is committed to a
sustainable future for our business, our readers
and our planet. This book is made from Forest
Stewardship Council® certified paper.

Contents

POSTHUMOUSLY PUBLISHED WORK

Introduction

by Linda Gray Sexton

Anne Sexton appointed me her literary executor in July of 1974, only three months before her suicide that October. She died just a few weeks short of her forty-fifth birthday. A ground-breaking American poet, she was a woman whose life was dominated on the one hand by a brilliance that won her the Pulitzer Prize, and on the other by a devastating and prolonged mental illness that ultimately killed her. Some called her a genius. I called her Mother.

I knew so little; I knew so much. Apparent to me even then was the sheer debilitating force of depression. After my birth in 1953, and then again after my sister's in 1955, my mother had two break-downs; she climbed aboard a roller-coaster ride of hospitalizations in various mental institutions, many of which were then punctuated by her meteoric successes within the world of American poetry, all between 1957 and 1974.

Born in Newton, Massachusetts in 1928, she was raised in a lax Episcopal household, the daughter of a prosperous wool merchant and a lady of leisure who supervised two maids and a cook. Anne was already a twenty-nine-year-old housewife when her first psychiatrist, Dr Martin Orne – who diagnosed her initially with postpartum depression and then later with the common catch-all of the time, 'hysteria' – recommended that as an antidote to depression she try writing poetry to help her grapple with her condition. His suggestion freed her, giving her licence to explore both her illness and her humanity, and soon a stack of poetry lay on her desk. Tentatively, but with singular artistry, she created a vivid portrait of the experiences undergone and the trials endured by psychiatric patients in the recesses of their own minds. Later, Orne would indicate to her that, if she were ever to publish her poems, the experiences she shared in them might help others to feel less alone.

Within months of writing her first verses, she enrolled herself in a poetry class in Boston. This was to be the first step of a journey that would bring her into contact with other writers just starting down the same path. Between them, they would forge a new kind of poetry: one tied intimately – and, by the standards of the time, brazenly and unapologetically – to the personal life of its author.

In the late 1950s, lyric verse in the United States was in the midst of a transformation, quite suddenly infused with a new and radical viewpoint, and Anne was at the crest of that wave. Until this time, poets had generally fashioned a formal and impersonal mask in their writing, from behind which they could speak without revealing their private lives. With the publication of Robert Lowell's *Life Studies* and W. D. Snodgrass's *Heart's Needle,* however, both in 1959, a new mode of poetry had rapidly begun to appear in American magazines, literary journals and, before long, in an increasing number of collections from major publishing houses. Dubbed 'confessional', it went far beyond the limitations previous generations had set for appropriate subject matter. Crossing the usual boundaries of propriety and reticence, and speaking frankly of the self, this kind of poetry took intimate emotions and events and made them into the source of its art. The literary community and the public consumed it with great eagerness, and soon psychiatrists began to recommend Anne's work to their patients as if referring them to a highly respected colleague.

She began to develop her own inimitable style at a pace that amazed those around her. Hunched over her manual typewriter as time sped by – sometimes late into the night after everyone else was in bed – she revised and revised each poem. Soon she had enough of them to fill a binder. Lightening her load as a housewife, a housekeeper provided by her mother did the cleaning and the laundry. Her mother-in-law took care of the children, supervising the schedule of daytime hours when we were infants and toddlers so that Anne could write and, as we grew into adolescence, shuttling us to ballroom dancing lessons and Glee Club practices.

Right from the start, my mother spent her late mornings through to 'cocktail hour' at her overloaded desk in the family room, pounding the keys of the typewriter and pressuring herself to improve. My father tried to encourage her, in spite of the precious time this writing carved from our family hours; on a deeper level, however, he failed to understand and began to resent her drive to create in rhythm and rhyme a poetry often deeply revealing of their private life.

And then, too, another pressure made itself felt: even as her horizons widened within the Boston poetry world, the battle with her interior voices continued, and her difficult sessions with Dr Orne also placed heavy demands on her time and attention. The psychological excavation required by therapy, which began initially with Dr Orne and then continued with a succession of psychiatrists over the years, gave her the material for the kind of poetry that would make her famous.

Robert Lowell took note of her work in 1958, and, despite her anxiety about being in a formal classroom, she began to study with him at Boston University. It was there, under his aegis, that Anne met Sylvia Plath, who was recently returned from Britain and likewise just beginning her journey down the road to phenomenal success. W. D. Snodgrass, Nolan Miller, George Starbuck, John Berryman and Maxine Kumin became compatriots in writing in the 'confessional mode'. All of them would influence her work for years to come.

Later in life, Anne would admit that she hated the term 'confessional', considering it reductive. In the early sixties, however, she stood shoulder-to-shoulder with the remarkable poets gathered under that aegis as, together and apart, they developed their own distinctive voices. Like them, she plunged into the topics eschewed by others who wrote in a more traditional fashion.

If you have never before read the work of Anne Sexton, you will now encounter a poet who speaks with an extraordinary courage and who delves into subjects marked off-limits in her time: childhood trauma and incest; drug and alcohol addiction; insanity and depression; masturbation and menstruation; marriage and adultery; motherhood, daughterhood and friendship; the longing to live and the longing to die. These are only some of the subjects she attacked, each one approached with fervor, ferocity and a simultaneous resounding clarity. Today this list of subjects may sound commonplace, but in the early sixties, in both the US and England alike, it was considered radical.

In short order came publication of her early poems in such places as *The Saturday Review*, *The New Yorker* and *Harper's Magazine*. In 1960, *To Bedlam and Partway Back* was published by the prestigious Houghton Mifflin Company, with *All My Pretty Ones* following shortly in 1962. Both garnered accolades. She had embarked.

Even as the 'confessional' label provided allies, however, Anne's participation in an intellectual community contributed to the anxieties that continued to beset her as she worked onwards in her therapy with Dr Orne. Her own lack of a serious education disturbed and haunted her; she had completed only a single year at a junior college – one which she always described to me as 'a finishing school where I learned to make the perfect white sauce'. No sooner had she begun to write than she began to read, scooping up everything from Henry James and Flaubert to Freud and Jung to combat her fear of being revealed as ignorant. Often she read more than one book at a time, dog-earing the pages and marking the margins with notes. No author was too tough to understand; no book was less than fascinating. In them she discovered another side of herself, and it was hungry for knowledge.

Self-educated though she was, her late career brought with it an invitation to lecture in creative writing at Boston University in 1970. There, despite the time it required her to spend away from her typewriter, she found that teaching young poets in a workshop setting brought her inspiration and invigorated her own work. In 1972, Colgate College offered her the Crashaw Chair in Literature with a full faculty position. She received several honorary doctoral degrees, an honorary Phi Beta Kappa from Harvard and many literary fellowships from respected institutions, as well as being named a fellow of The Royal Society of Literature in Great Britain.

It must be said that, although Anne Sexton's writing appealed to women in particular, her wide-ranging topics always included men. She never labelled herself a 'feminist', but her fruitful career did indeed break through her assigned role as a 'housewife' in the fifties and early sixties, a time during which women were often expected to limit themselves to motherhood, to the cooking of meatloaf and to the washing of laundry – sometimes with pleasure, but at other times with a sense of claustrophobia and isolation. In her copy of the groundbreaking *The Feminine Mystique* by the American author Betty Friedan, Anne underlined so hard with her pencil that the page was scored, as she wrote repeatedly in the margin 'This is *me! Me!*' Breaking free of all that Friedan decried, she set an example for others who also needed escape from the traditional stereotypes of that decade. She spoke for women, and women spoke back.

Had you met my mother at a cocktail party, you would have been struck by her beauty and vivacity, as well as by the vulnerability that lay beneath her smile when you looked closely enough. Witty and charming, she could captivate a room, and at the height of her career during public readings of her poetry – always jam-packed – she utterly captured her audience's attentions. Dressed seductively and gesturing with her graceful arms and hands, she spoke in a low, throaty rasp. Everything about her spelled sensuality, and yet she brought to the men and women gathered there an art that stunned with its seriousness as well as its drama. She was always anxious about appearing in public, but she concealed it well and usually ended on a high note – as, for example, in her later years, with a poem like 'The Rowing Endeth'. A standing ovation was nearly always her reward.

Anne began to offer advice and assistance to a new generation of poets and writers in whom she saw talent: Erica Jong, C. K. Williams and Mary Gordon, all of whom would go on to the successes she had foreseen when they'd first written to her with samples of their work. Among her professional friends and confederates she now counted Ted Hughes, John Cheever, Kurt Vonnegut, John Malcolm Brinnin, James Dickey, Joyce Carol Oates, May Swenson, Donald Hall, Stanley Kunitz and others. Her experience in the 'business of words', as she was fond of calling it, was expanding.

Following the publication of *Live or Die* in 1966, which won her the Pulitzer a year later, and *Love Poems* in 1969, the rough, taboo soil she had trodden so uncertainly to begin with became a smoother path. The poetry wasn't so startling any more, perhaps either for herself or for her readers; and by mid-career she was seeking something different to inspire her. Always motivated to bring new material before her readers, she chose the unconscious horror of the fairy tale to supplant the obvious horror of the mental institution. In 1970, she submitted to Houghton Mifflin her *Transformations*, which reinterpreted the tales of the Brothers Grimm in poems glittering with a dark sense of humour; this humour – however black – had always been part of her outlook, despite the troubles of her life, and now she pulled it into her work. Houghton Mifflin was uneasy about the departure from her usual style but, at Anne's insistence, published the book in 1971. It went on to be one of her most popular volumes.

Lively as it was, however, *Transformations* would not ultimately sustain her. Little by little, as the years passed, friends, family and a succession of new psychiatrists began to draw back from the storm surge of Anne's illness and the alcoholism she would never defeat. In the years before her suicide, Anne increasingly turned for comfort to a God of her own making. She wrote extensively about Jesus, angels and religion in *The Book of Folly* (1972) and, perhaps most notably, in the psalms gathered as 'O Ye Tongues' in the last volume of her poetry published while she was alive, *The Death Notebooks* (1974).

Her focus on religion culminated in *The Awful Rowing Toward God,* which would be published posthumously in 1975. Raw, powerful, and written in what Maxine Kumin called 'a white heat' over only a few weeks, it stood as the final word from a woman who had nicknamed herself 'Ms Dog' – a palindrome for 'God'. She looked for him, her, or it anywhere and everywhere in these last years. When madness and alcoholism were beating down the door, she took solace in the idea that, somewhere and sometime, a benevolent being would grant her comfort before all else failed.

She did not stop writing in the months before her suicide, and produced more poetry about her drive toward some kind of belief; these poems I gathered together and published posthumously, after I had had time to consider what course she would have taken on her own. In 1976 and 1978, respectively, I edited *45 Mercy Street* and *Words for Dr. Y.* in tandem with her editor at Houghton Mifflin. Both were published to fanfare, along with a number of *Last Poems* that we deemed of interest and mastery, though she had not yet decided to bring them out into the world. All three of these final collections, so often marked by her increasing reach toward religion, were included in *The Complete Poems* in 1981.

In her final years, increasingly alone and alienated from the family and friends to whom she had failed to remain close, Anne envisioned God as a woman who would provide her with shelter and love. Some time in April, just six months before her death, when the pace of her writing began to slow, 'In Excelsis' rolled out of her typewriter. Written to her last therapist – a woman whom she came to love and depend upon – the poem envisions the two of them standing at the edge of the ocean and captures her longing for a divine and empathetic woman who will grant her the serenity she has craved for so many years, as well as the succour that lies deep within the sea's 'great mother arms'. Entering the waves 'like a dream', she leaves her past behind her on the shore and wades out to embrace the current. 'In Excelsis' speaks to her life's last hunger, and for this volume to close with it seems apposite.

Despite her Episcopal origins, her longing for a religion that relied on both ceremony and ritual drew her to Catholicism; in the end, however, a priest from whom she begged absolution told her that because she was not of the faith, he could neither listen to her confession nor administer the last rites. Nevertheless, he reassured her, she had no need of either. 'God is in your typewriter,' he told her, much as Dr Orne had once said that health could be found in the exact same place.

It is no exaggeration to say that even then, in 1974, the challenge Dr Orne had posed to her some twenty-six years before had been met. When she killed herself, Anne Sexton left behind not only a grieving family, but thousands more 'common readers' who had been made to feel less alone because of her work, and who were bereft at her suicide. And an admiring public remains hungry even now for her bold aesthetic. As both her daughter and her literary executor, I am inundated with requests from those who wish to reach out to me because I was so close to her; they bare their lives and souls to me, just as she had once dared to bare hers to them. Readers of this book may feel that they, too, have come to know Anne Sexton as well as her intimates did, so much does every poem reverberate with the stamp of her life.

That October brought an end to the life of a troubled woman who had helped to change the face of American poetry in two short decades, and the American literary community mourned the premature loss of her genius. Ultimately, though, it was the poetry that had saved her for so many years, and it is the poetry that remains with us. Today, her work has been published around the globe, translated into over thirty languages and set to music in both opera and rock, as well being made into numerous dramatic productions; it is anthologized widely and taught in high schools and universities throughout the world. Through her work we can take comfort in spite of our loss: through her work we can continue to listen to a woman who spoke with candour and thus transformed the world of poetry in her time.

On the day she appointed me her literary executor, she wrote me a letter in which she confided one final hope: 'Maybe, just maybe, the spirit of the poems will go on past both of us, and one or two will be remembered in one hundred years . . . and maybe not.' Despite her doubts about the endurance of her legacy, this last wish has been fulfilled. Her poetry certainly will be remembered for one hundred years – and more. She will live on.

Mercies

The Balance Wheel

Where I waved at the sky
And waited your love through a February sleep,
I saw birds swinging in, watched them multiply
Into a tree, weaving on a branch, cradling a keep
In the arms of April, sprung from the south to occupy
This slow lap of land, like cogs of some balance wheel.
I saw them build the air, with that motion birds feel.

Where I wave at the sky
And understand love, knowing our August heat,
I see birds pulling past the dim frosted thigh
Of Autumn, unlatched from the nest, and wing-beat
For the south, making their high dots across the sky,
Like beauty spots marking a still perfect cheek.
I see them bend the air, slipping away, for what birds seek.

from *To Bedlam and Part Way Back*

(1960)

You, Doctor Martin

You, Doctor Martin, walk
from breakfast to madness. Late August,
I speed through the antiseptic tunnel
          where the moving dead still talk
of pushing their bones against the thrust
of cure. And I am queen of this summer hotel
          or the laughing bee on a stalk

of death. We stand in broken
lines and wait while they unlock
the door and count us at the frozen gates
          of dinner. The shibboleth is spoken
and we move to gravy in our smock
of smiles. We chew in rows, our plates
          scratch and whine like chalk

in school. There are no knives
for cutting your throat. I make
moccasins all morning. At first my hands
          kept empty, unraveled for the lives
they used to work. Now I learn to take
them back, each angry finger that demands
          I mend what another will break

tomorrow. Of course, I love you;
you lean above the plastic sky,
god of our block, prince of all the foxes.
          The breaking crowns are new
that Jack wore. Your third eye
moves among us and lights the separate boxes
          where we sleep or cry.

What large children we are
here. All over I grow most tall
in the best ward. Your business is people,
          you call at the madhouse, an oracular
eye in our nest. Out in the hall
the intercom pages you. You twist in the pull
          of the foxy children who fall

          like floods of life in frost.
And we are magic talking to itself,
noisy and alone. I am queen of all my sins
          forgotten. Am I still lost?
Once I was beautiful. Now I am myself,
counting this row and that row of moccasins
          waiting on the silent shelf.

Music Swims Back to Me

Wait Mister. Which way is home?
They turned the light out
and the dark is moving in the corner.
There are no sign posts in this room,
four ladies, over eighty,
in diapers every one of them.
La la la, Oh music swims back to me
and I can feel the tune they played
the night they left me
in this private institution on a hill.

Imagine it. A radio playing
and everyone here was crazy.
I liked it and danced in a circle.
Music pours over the sense
and in a funny way
music sees more than I.
I mean it remembers better;
remembers the first night here.
It was the strangled cold of November;
even the stars were strapped in the sky
and that moon too bright
forking through the bars to stick me
with a singing in the head.
I have forgotten all the rest.

They lock me in this chair at eight a.m.
and there are no signs to tell the way,
just the radio beating to itself
and the song that remembers

more than I. Oh, la la la,
this music swims back to me.
The night I came I danced a circle
and was not afraid.
Mister?

Said the Poet to the Analyst

My business is words. Words are like labels,
or coins, or better, like swarming bees.
I confess I am only broken by the sources of things;
as if words were counted like dead bees in the attic,
unbuckled from their yellow eyes and their dry wings.
I must always forget how one word is able to pick
out another, to manner another, until I have got
something I might have said . . .
but did not.

Your business is watching my words. But I
admit nothing. I work with my best, for instance,
when I can write my praise for a nickel machine,
that one night in Nevada: telling how the magic jackpot
came clacking three bells out, over the lucky screen.

But if you should say this is something it is not,
then I grow weak, remembering how my hands felt funny
and ridiculous and crowded with all
the believing money.

Her Kind

I have gone out, a possessed witch,
haunting the black air, braver at night;
dreaming evil, I have done my hitch
over the plain houses, light by light:
lonely thing, twelve-fingered, out of mind.
A women like that is not a woman, quite.
I have been her kind.

I have found the warm caves in the woods,
filled them with skillets, carvings, shelves,
closets, silks, innumerable goods;
fixed the suppers for the worms and the elves:
whining, rearranging the disaligned.
A woman like that is misunderstood.
I have been her kind.

I have ridden in your cart, driver,
waved my nude arms at villages going by,
learning the last bright routes, survivor
where your flames still bite my thigh
and my ribs crack where your wheels wind.
A woman like that is not ashamed to die.
I have been her kind.

Unknown Girl in the Maternity Ward

Child, the current of your breath is six days long.
You lie, a small knuckle on my white bed;
lie, fisted like a snail, so small and strong
at my breast. Your lips are animals; you are fed
with love. At first hunger is not wrong.
The nurses nod their caps; you are shepherded
down starch halls with the other unnested throng
in wheeling baskets. You tip like a cup; your head
moving to my touch. You sense the way we belong.
But this is an institution bed.
You will not know me very long.

The doctors are enamel. They want to know
the facts. They guess about the man who left me,
some pendulum soul, going the way men go
and leave you full of child. But our case history
stays blank. All I did was let you grow.
Now we are here for all the ward to see.
They thought I was strange, although
I never spoke a word. I burst empty
of you, letting you learn how the air is so.
The doctors chart the riddle they ask of me
and I turn my head away. I do not know.

Yours is the only face I recognize.
Bone at my bone, you drink my answers in.
Six times a day I prize
your need, the animals of your lips, your skin
growing warm and plump. I see your eyes
lifting their tents. They are blue stones, they begin

to outgrow their moss. You blink in surprise
and I wonder what you can see, my funny kin,
as you trouble my silence. I am a shelter of lies.
Should I learn to speak again, or hopeless in
such sanity will I touch some face I recognize?

Down the hall the baskets start back. My arms
fit you like a sleeve, they hold
catkins of your willows, the wild bee farms
of your nerves, each muscle and fold
of your first days. Your old man's face disarms
the nurses. But the doctors return to scold
me. I speak. It is you my silence harms.
I should have known; I should have told
them something to write down. My voice alarms
my throat. 'Name of father – none.' I hold
you and name you bastard in my arms.

And now that's that. There is nothing more
that I can say or lose.
Others have traded life before
and could not speak. I tighten to refuse
your owling eyes, my fragile visitor.
I touch your cheeks, like flowers. You bruise
against me. We unlearn. I am a shore
rocking you off. You break from me. I choose
your only way, my small inheritor
and hand you off, trembling the selves we lose.
Go child, who is my sin and nothing more.

For John, Who Begs Me Not to Enquire Further

Not that it was beautiful,
but that, in the end, there was
a certain sense of order there;
something worth learning
in that narrow diary of my mind,
in the commonplaces of the asylum
where the cracked mirror
or my own selfish death
outstared me.
And if I tried
to give you something else,
something outside of myself,
you would not know
that the worst of anyone
can be, finally,
an accident of hope.
I tapped my own head;
it was glass, an inverted bowl!.
It is a small thing
to rage in your own bowl.
At first it was private.
Then it was more than myself;
it was you, or your house
or your kitchen.
And if you turn away
because there is no lesson here
I will hold my awkward bowl,
with all its cracked stars shining
like a complicated lie,
and fasten a new skin around it

as if I were dressing an orange
or a strange sun.
Not that it was beautiful,
but that I found some order there.
There ought to be something special
for someone
in this kind of hope.
This is something I would never find
in a lovelier place, my dear,
although your fear is anyone's fear,
like an invisible veil between us all . . .
and sometimes in private,
my kitchen, your kitchen,
my face, your face.

Some Foreign Letters

I knew you forever and you were always old,
soft white lady of my heart. Surely you would scold
me for sitting up late, reading your letters,
as if these foreign postmarks were meant for me.
You posted them first in London, wearing furs
and a new dress in the winter of eighteen-ninety.
I read how London is dull on Lord Mayor's Day,
where you guided past groups of robbers, the sad holes
of Whitechapel, clutching your pocketbook, on the way
to Jack the Ripper dissecting his famous bones.
This Wednesday in Berlin, you say, you will
go to a bazaar at Bismarck's house. And I
see you as a young girl in a good world still,
writing three generations before mine. I try
to reach into your page and breathe it back . . .
but life is a trick, life is a kitten in a sack.

This is the sack of time your death vacates.
How distant you are on your nickel-plated skates
in the skating park in Berlin, gliding past
me with your Count, while a military band
plays a Strauss waltz. I loved you last,
a pleated old lady with a crooked hand.
Once you read *Lohengrin* and every goose
hung high while you practiced castle life
in Hanover. Tonight your letters reduce
history to a guess. The Count had a wife.
You were the old maid aunt who lived with us.
Tonight I read how the winter howled around
the towers of Schloss Schwöbber, how the tedious

language grew in your jaw, how you loved the sound
of the music of the rats tapping on the stone
floors. When you were mine you wore an earphone.

This is Wednesday, May 9th, near Lucerne,
Switzerland, sixty-nine years ago. I learn
your first climb up Mount San Salvatore;
this is the rocky path, the hole in your shoes,
the yankee girl, the iron interior
of her sweet body. You let the Count choose
your next climb. You went together, armed
with alpine stocks, with ham sandwiches
and seltzer wasser. You were not alarmed
by the thick woods of briars and bushes,
nor the rugged cliff, nor the first vertigo
up over Lake Lucerne. The Count sweated
with his coat off as you waded through top snow.
He held your hand and kissed you. You rattled
down on the train to catch a steamboat for home;
or other postmarks: Paris, Verona, Rome.

This is Italy. You learn its mother tongue.
I read how you walked on the Palatine among
the ruins of the palaces of the Caesars;
alone in the Roman autumn, alone since July.
When you were mine they wrapped you out of here
with your best hat over your face. I cried
because I was seventeen. I am older now.
I read how your student ticket admitted you
into the private chapel of the Vatican and how
you cheered with the others, as we used to do
on the Fourth of July. One Wednesday in November
you watched a balloon, painted like a silver ball,
float up over the Forum, up over the lost emperors,
to shiver its little modern cage in an occasional
breeze. You worked your New England conscience out
beside artisans, chestnut vendors and the devout.

Tonight I will learn to love you twice;
learn your first days, your mid-Victorian face.
Tonight I will speak up and interrupt
your letters, warning you that wars are coming,
that the Count will die, that you will accept
your America back to live like a prim thing
on the farm in Maine. I tell you, you will come
here, to the suburbs of Boston, to see the blue-nose
world go drunk each night, to see the handsome
children jitterbug, to feel your left ear close
one Friday at Symphony. And I tell you,
you will tip your boot feet out of that hall,
rocking from its sour sound, out onto
the crowded street, letting your spectacles fall
and your hair net tangle as you stop passers-by
to mumble your guilty love while your ears die.

The Double Image

1.

I am thirty this November.
You are still small, in your fourth year.
We stand watching the yellow leaves go queer,
flapping in the winter rain,
falling flat and washed. And I remember
mostly the three autumns you did not live here.
They said I'd never get you back again.
I tell you what you'll never really know:
all the medical hypothesis
that explained my brain will never be as true as these
struck leaves letting go.

I, who chose two times
to kill myself, had said your nickname
the mewling months when you first came;
until a fever rattled
in your throat and I moved like a pantomime
above your head. Ugly angels spoke to me. The blame,
I heard them say, was mine. They tattled
like green witches in my head, letting doom
leak like a broken faucet;
as if doom had flooded my belly and filled your bassinet,
an old debt I must assume.

Death was simpler than I'd thought.
The day life made you well and whole
I let the witches take away my guilty soul.
I pretended I was dead

until the white men pumped the poison out,
putting me armless and washed through the rigamarole
of talking boxes and the electric bed.
I laughed to see the private iron in that hotel.
Today the yellow leaves
go queer. You ask me where they go. I say today believed
in itself, or else it fell.

Today, my small child, Joyce,
love your self's self where it lives.
There is no special God to refer to; or if there is,
why did I let you grow
in another place. You did not know my voice
when I came back to call. All the superlatives
of tomorrow's white tree and mistletoe
will not help you know the holidays you had to miss.
The time I did not love
myself, I visited your shoveled walks; you held my glove.
There was new snow after this.

2.

They sent me letters with news
of you and I made moccasins that I would never use.
When I grew well enough to tolerate
myself, I lived with my mother. Too late,
too late, to live with your mother, the witches said.
But I didn't leave. I had my portrait
done instead.

Part way back from Bedlam
I came to my mother's house in Gloucester,
Massachusetts. And this is how I came
to catch at her; and this is how I lost her.
I cannot forgive your suicide, my mother said.
And she never could. She had my portrait
done instead.

I lived like an angry guest,
like a partly mended thing, an outgrown child.
I remember my mother did her best.
She took me to Boston and had my hair restyled.
Your smile is like your mother's, the artist said.
I didn't seem to care. I had my portrait
done instead.

There was a church where I grew up
with its white cupboards where they locked us up,
row by row, like puritans or shipmates
singing together. My father passed the plate.
Too late to be forgiven now, the witches said.
I wasn't exactly forgiven. They had my portrait
done instead.

3.

All that summer sprinklers arched
over the seaside grass.
We talked of drought
while the salt-parched
field grew sweet again. To help time pass
I tried to mow the lawn
and in the morning I had my portrait done,
holding my smile in place, till it grew formal.
Once I mailed you a picture of a rabbit
and a postcard of Motif number one,
as if it were normal
to be a mother and be gone.

They hung my portrait in the chill
north light, matching
me to keep me well.
Only my mother grew ill.
She turned from me, as if death were catching,

as if death transferred,
as if my dying had eaten inside of her.
That August you were two, but I timed my days with doubt.
On the first of September she looked at me
and said I gave her cancer.
They carved her sweet hills out
and still I couldn't answer.

4.

That winter she came
part way back
from her sterile suite
of doctors, the seasick
cruise of the X-ray,
the cells' arithmetic
gone wild. Surgery incomplete,
the fat arm, the prognosis poor, I heard
them say.

During the sea blizzards
she had her
own portrait painted.
A cave of a mirror
placed on the south wall;
matching smile, matching contour.
And you resembled me; unacquainted
with my face, you wore it. But you were mine
after all.

I wintered in Boston,
childless bride,
nothing sweet to spare
with witches at my side.
I missed your babyhood,
tried a second suicide,

tried the sealed hotel a second year.
On April Fool you fooled me. We laughed and this
was good.

5.

I checked out for the last time
on the first of May;
graduate of the mental cases,
with my analyst's okay,
my complete book of rhymes,
my typewriter and my suitcases.

All that summer I learned life
back into my own
seven rooms, visited the swan boats,
the market, answered the phone,
served cocktails as a wife
should, made love among my petticoats

and August tan. And you came each
weekend. But I lie.
You seldom came. I just pretended
you, small piglet, butterfly
girl with jelly bean cheeks,
disobedient three, my splendid

stranger. And I had to learn
why I would rather
die than love, how your innocence
would hurt and how I gather
guilt like a young intern
his symptoms, his certain evidence.

That October day we went
to Gloucester the red hills
reminded me of the dry red fur fox
coat I played in as a child; stock-still
like a bear or a tent,
like a great cave laughing or a red fur fox.

We drove past the hatchery,
the hut that sells bait,
past Pigeon Cove, past the Yacht Club, past Squall's
Hill, to the house that waits
still, on the top of the sea,
and two portraits hang on opposite walls.

6.

In north light, my smile is held in place,
the shadow marks my bone.
What could I have been dreaming as I sat there,
all of me waiting in the eyes, the zone
of the smile, the young face,
the foxes' snare.

In south light, her smile is held in place,
her cheeks wilting like a dry
orchid; my mocking mirror, my overthrown
love, my first image. She eyes me from that face,
that stony head of death
I had outgrown.

The artist caught us at the turning;
we smiled in our canvas home
before we chose our foreknown separate ways.
The dry red fur fox coat was made for burning.
I rot on the wall, my own
Dorian Gray.

And this was the cave of the mirror,
that double woman who stares
at herself, as if she were petrified
in time – two ladies sitting in umber chairs.
You kissed your grandmother
and she cried.

7.

I could not get you back
except for weekends. You came
each time, clutching the picture of a rabbit
that I had sent you. For the last time I unpack
your things. We touch from habit.
The first visit you asked my name.
Now you stay for good. I will forget
how we bumped away from each other like marionettes
on strings. It wasn't the same
as love, letting weekends contain
us. You scrape your knee. You learn my name,
wobbling up the sidewalk, calling and crying.
You call me mother and I remember my mother again,
somewhere in greater Boston, dying.

I remember we named you Joyce
so we could call you Joy.
You came like an awkward guest
that first time, all wrapped and moist
and strange at my heavy breast.
I needed you. I didn't want a boy,
only a girl, a small milky mouse
of a girl, already loved, already loud in the house
of herself. We named you Joy.
I, who was never quite sure
about being a girl, needed another

life, another image to remind me.
And this was my worst guilt; you could not cure
nor soothe it. I made you to find me.

The Division of Parts

1.

Mother, my Mary Gray,
once resident of Gloucester
and Essex Country,
a photostat of your will
arrived in the mail today.
This is the division of money.
I am one third
of your daughters counting my bounty
or I am a queen alone
in the parlor still,
eating the bread and honey.
It is Good Friday.
Black birds pick at my window sill.

Your coat in my closet,
your bright stones on my hand,
the gaudy fur animals
I do not know how to use,
settle on me like a debt.
A week ago, while the hard March gales
beat on your house,
we sorted your things: obstacles
of letters, family silver,
eyeglasses and shoes.
Like some unseasoned Christmas, its scales
rigged and reset,
I bundled out with gifts I did not choose.

Now the hours of The Cross
rewind. In Boston, the devout
work their cold knees
toward that sweet martyrdom
that Christ planned. My timely loss
is too customary to note; and yet
I planned to suffer
and I cannot. It does not please
my yankee bones to watch
where the dying is done
in its ugly hours. Black birds peck
at my window glass
and Easter will take its ragged son.

The clutter of worship
that you taught me, Mary Gray,
is old. I imitate
a memory of belief
that I do not own. I trip
on your death and Jesus, my stranger
floats up over
my Christian home, wearing his straight
thorn tree. I have cast my lot
and am one third thief
of you. Time, that rearranger
of estates, equips
me with your garments, but not with grief.

2.

This winter when
cancer began its ugliness
I grieved with you each day
for three months
and found you in your private nook
of the medicinal palace

for New England Women
and never once
forgot how long it took.

I read to you
from *The New Yorker*, ate suppers
you wouldn't eat, fussed
with your flowers,
joked with your nurses, as if I
were the balm among lepers,
as if I could undo
a life in hours
if I never said goodbye.

But you turned old,
all your fifty-eight years sliding
like masks from your skull;
and at the end
I packed your nightgowns in suitcases,
paid the nurses, came riding
home as if I'd been told
I could pretend
people live in places.

3.

Since then I have pretended ease,
loved with the trickeries of need, but not enough
to shed my daughterhood
or sweeten him as a man.
I drink the five o'clock martinis
and poke at this dry page like a rough
goat. Fool! I fumble my lost childhood
for a mother and lounge in sad stuff
with love to catch and catch as catch can.

And Christ still waits. I have tried
to exorcise the memory of each event
and remain still, a mixed child,
heavy with cloths of you.
Sweet witch, you are my worried guide.
Such dangerous angels walk through Lent.
Their walls creak *Anne! Convert! Convert!*
My desk moves. Its cave murmurs Boo
and I am taken and beguiled.

Or wrong. For all the way I've come
I'll have to go again. Instead, I must convert
to love as reasonable
as Latin, as solid as earthenware:
an equilibrium
I never knew. And Lent will keep its hurt
for someone else. Christ knows enough
staunch guys have hitched on him in trouble,
thinking his sticks were badges to wear.

4.

Spring rusts on its skinny branch
and last summer's lawn
is soggy and brown.
Yesterday is just a number.
All of its winters avalanche
out of sight. What was, is gone.
Mother, last night I slept
in your Bonwit Teller nightgown.
Divided, you climbed into my head.
There in my jabbering dream
I heard my own angry cries
and I cursed you, *Dame*
keep out of my slumber.

My good Dame, you are dead.
And Mother, three stones
slipped from your glittering eyes.

Now it is Friday's noon
and I would still curse
you with my rhyming words
and bring you flapping back, old love,
old circus knitting, god-in-her-moon,
all fairest in my lang syne verse,
the gauzy bride among the children,
the fancy amid the absurd
and awkward, that horn for hounds
that skipper homeward, that museum
keeper of stiff starfish, that blaze
within the pilgrim woman,
a clown mender, a dove's
cheek among the stones,
my Lady of my first words,
this is the division of ways.

And now, while Christ stays
fastened to his Crucifix
so that love may praise
his sacrifice
and not the grotesque metaphor,
you come, a brave ghost, to fix
in my mind without praise
or paradise
to make me your inheritor.

from *All My Pretty Ones*

(1962)

All My Pretty Ones

Father, this year's jinx rides us apart
where you followed our mother to her cold slumber;
a second shock boiling its stone to your heart,
leaving me here to shuffle and disencumber
you from the residence you could not afford:
a gold key, your half of a woolen mill,
twenty suits from Dunne's, an English Ford,
the love and legal verbiage of another will,
boxes of pictures of people I do not know.
I touch their cardboard faces. They must go.

But the eyes, as thick as wood in this album,
hold me. I stop here, where a small boy
waits in a ruffled dress for someone to come . . .
for this soldier who holds his bugle like a toy
or for this velvet lady who cannot smile.
Is this your father's father, this commodore
in a mailman suit? My father, time meanwhile
has made it unimportant who you are looking for.
I'll never know what these faces are all about.
I lock them into their book and throw them out.

This is the yellow scrapbook that you began
the year I was born; as crackling now and wrinkly
as tobacco leaves: clippings where Hoover outran
the Democrats, wiggling his dry finger at me
and Prohibition; news where the *Hindenburg* went
down and recent years where you went flush
on war. This year, solvent but sick, you meant

to marry that pretty widow in a one-month rush.
But before you had that second chance, I cried
on your fat shoulder. Three days later you died.

These are the snapshots of marriage, stopped in places.
Side by side at the rail toward Nassau now;
here, with the winner's cup at the speedboat races,
here, in tails at the Cotillion, you take a bow,
here, by our kennel of dogs with their pink eyes,
running like show-bred pigs in their chain-link pen;
here, at the horseshow where my sister wins a prize;
and here, standing like a duke among groups of men.
Now I fold you down, my drunkard, my navigator,
my first lost keeper, to love or look at later.

I hold a five-year diary that my mother kept
for three years, telling all she does not say
of your alcoholic tendency. You overslept,
she writes. My God, father, each Christmas Day
with your blood, will I drink down your glass
of wine? The diary of your hurly-burly years
goes to my shelf to wait for my age to pass.
Only in this hoarded span will love persevere.
Whether you are pretty or not, I outlive you,
bend down my strange face to yours and forgive you.

The Truth the Dead Know

For my mother, born March 1902, died March 1959
and my father, born February 1900, died June 1959

Gone, I say and walk from church,
refusing the stiff procession to the grave,
letting the dead ride alone in the hearse.
It is June. I am tired of being brave.

We drive to the Cape. I cultivate
myself where the sun gutters from the sky,
where the sea swings in like an iron gate
and we touch. In another country people die.

My darling, the wind falls in like stones
from the whitehearted water and when we touch
we enter touch entirely. No one's alone.
Men kill for this, or for as much.

And what of the dead? They lie without shoes
in their stone boats. They are more like stone
than the sea would be if it stopped. They refuse
to be blessed, throat, eye and knucklebone.

Young

A thousand doors ago
when I was a lonely kid
in a big house with four
garages and it was summer
as long as I could remember,
I lay on the lawn at night,
clover wrinkling under me,
the wise stars bedding over me,
my mother's window a funnel
of yellow heat running out,
my father's window, half shut,
an eye where sleepers pass,
and the boards of the house
were smooth and white as wax
and probably a million leaves
sailed on their strange stalks
as the crickets ticked together
and I, in my brand new body,
which was not a woman's yet,
told the stars my questions
and thought God could really see
the heat and the painted light,
elbows, knees, dreams, goodnight.

I Remember

By the first of August
the invisible beetles began
to snore and the grass was
as tough as hemp and was
no color – no more than
the sand was a color and
we had worn our bare feet
bare since the twentieth
of June and there were times
we forgot to wind up your
alarm clock and some nights
we took our gin warm and neat
from old jelly glasses while
the sun blew out of sight
like a red picture hat and
one day I tied my hair back
with a ribbon and you said
that I looked almost like
a puritan lady and what
I remember best is that
the door to your room was
the door to mine.

The Operation

1.

After the sweet promise,
the summer's mild retreat
from mother's cancer, the winter months of her death,
I come to this white office, its sterile sheet,
its hard tablet, its stirrups, to hold my breath
while I, who must, allow the glove its oily rape,
to hear the almost mighty doctor over me equate
my ills with hers
and decide to operate.

It grew in her
as simply as a child would grow,
as simply as she housed me once, fat and female.
Always my most gentle house before that embryo
of evil spread in her shelter and she grew frail.
Frail, we say, remembering fear, that face we wear
in the room of the special smells of dying, fear
where the snoring mouth gapes
and is not dear.

There was snow everywhere.
Each day I grueled through
its sloppy peak, its blue-struck days, my boots
slapping into the hospital halls, past the retinue
of nurses at the desk, to murmur in cahoots
with hers outside her door, to enter with the outside
air stuck on my skin, to enter smelling her pride,

her upkeep, and to lie
as all who love have lied.

No reason to be afraid,
my almost mighty doctor reasons.
I nod, thinking that woman's dying
must come in seasons,
thinking that living is worth buying.
I walk out, scuffing a raw leaf,
kicking the clumps of dead straw
that were this summer's lawn.
Automatically I get in my car,
knowing the historic thief
is loose in my house
and must be set upon.

2.

Clean of the body's hair,
I lie smooth from breast to leg.
All that was special, all that was rare
is common here. Fact: death too is in the egg.
Fact: the body is dumb, the body is meat.
And tomorrow the O.R. Only the summer was sweet.

The rooms down the hall are calling
all night long, while the night outside
sucks at the trees. I hear limbs falling
and see yellow eyes flick in the rain. Wide eyed
and still whole I turn in my bin like a shorn lamb.
A nurse's flashlight blinds me to see who I am.

The walls color in a wash
of daylight until the room takes its objects
into itself again. I smoke furtively and squash

the butt and hide it with my watch and other effects.
The halls bustle with legs. I smile at the nurse
who smiles for the morning shift. Day is worse.

Scheduled late, I cannot drink
or eat, except for yellow pills
and a jigger of water. I wait and think
until she brings two mysterious needles: the skills
she knows she knows, promising, soon you'll be out.
But nothing is sure. No one. I wait in doubt.

I wait like a kennel of dogs
jumping against their fence. At ten
she returns, laughs and catalogues
my resistance to drugs. On the stretcher, citizen
and boss of my own body still, I glide down the halls
and rise in the iron cage toward science and pitfalls.

The great green people stand
over me; I roll on the table
under a terrible sun, following their command
to curl, head touching knee if I am able.
Next, I am hung up like a saddle and they begin.
Pale as an angel I float out over my own skin.

I soar in hostile air
over the pure women in labor,
over the crowning heads of babies being born.
I plunge down the backstair
calling *mother* at the dying door,
to rush back to my own skin, tied where it was torn.
Its nerves pull like wires
snapping from the leg to the rib.
Strangers, their faces rolling like hoops, require
my arm. I am lifted into my aluminum crib.

3.

Skull flat, here in my harness,
thick with shock, I call mother
to help myself, call toe of frog,
that woolly bat, that tongue of dog;
call God help and all the rest.
The soul that swam the furious water
sinks now in flies and the brain
flops like a docked fish and the eyes
are flat boat decks riding out the pain.

My nurses, those starchy ghosts,
hover over me for my lame hours
and my lame days. The mechanics
of the body pump for their tricks.
I rest on their needles, am dosed
and snoring amid the orange flowers
and the eyes of visitors. I wear,
like some senile woman, a scarlet
candy package ribbon in my hair.

Four days from home I lurk on my
mechanical parapet with two pillows
at my elbows, as soft as praying cushions.
My knees work with the bed that runs
on power. I grumble to forget the lie
I ought to hear, but don't. God knows
I thought I'd die – but here I am,
recalling mother, the sound of her
good morning, the odor of orange and jam.

All's well, they say. They say I'm better.
I lounge in frills or, picturesque,
I wear bunny pink slippers in the hall.

I read a new book and shuffle past the desk
to mail the author my first fan letter.
Time now to pack this humpty-dumpty
back the frightened way she came
and run along, Anne, and run along now,
my stomach laced up like a football
for the game.

A Curse Against Elegies

Oh, love, why do we argue like this?
I am tired of all your pious talk.
Also, I am tired of all the dead.
They refuse to listen,
so leave them alone.
Take your foot out of the graveyard,
they are busy being dead.

Everyone was always to blame:
the last empty fifth of booze,
the rusty nails and chicken feathers
that stuck in the mud on the back doorstep,
the worms that lived under the cat's ear
and the thin-lipped preacher
who refused to call
except once on a flea-ridden day
when he came scuffing in through the yard
looking for a scapegoat.
I hid in the kitchen under the ragbag.

I refuse to remember the dead.
And the dead are bored with the whole thing.
But you – you go ahead,
go on, go on back down
into the graveyard,
lie down where you think their faces are;
talk back to your old bad dreams.

Housewife

Some women marry houses.
It's another kind of skin; it has a heart,
a mouth, a liver and bowel movements.
The walls are permanent and pink.
See how she sits on her knees all day,
faithfully washing herself down.
Men enter by force, drawn back like Jonah
into their fleshy mothers.
A woman *is* her mother.
That's the main thing.

The Fortress

while taking a nap with Linda

Under the pink quilted covers
I hold the pulse that counts your blood.
I think the woods outdoors
are half asleep,
left over from summer
like a stack of books after a flood,
left over like those promises I never keep.
On the right, the scrub pine tree
waits like a fruit store
holding up bunches of tufted broccoli.

We watch the wind from our square bed.
I press down my index finger –
half in jest, half in dread –
on the brown mole
under your left eye, inherited
from my right cheek: a spot of danger
where a bewitched worm ate its way through our soul
in search of beauty. My child, since July
the leaves have been fed
secretly from a pool of beet-red dye.

And sometimes they are battle green
with trunks as wet as hunters' boots,
smacked hard by the wind, clean
as oilskins. No,
the wind's not off the ocean.
Yes, it cried in your room like a wolf
and your pony tail hurt you. That was a long time ago.

47

The wind rolled the tide like a dying
woman. She wouldn't sleep,
she rolled there all night, grunting and sighing.

Darling, life is not in my hands;
life with its terrible changes
will take you, bombs or glands,
your own child at
your breast, your own house on your own land.
Outside the bittersweet turns orange.
Before she died, my mother and I picked those fat
branches, finding orange nipples
on the gray wire strands.
We weeded the forest, curing trees like cripples.

Your feet thump-thump against my back
and you whisper to yourself. Child,
what are you wishing? What pact
are you making?
What mouse runs between your eyes? What ark
can I fill for you when the world goes wild?
The woods are underwater, their weeds are shaking
in the tide; birches like zebra fish
flash by in a pack.
Child, I cannot promise that you will get your wish.

I cannot promise very much.
I give you the images I know.
Lie still with me and watch.
A pheasant moves
by like a seal, pulled through the mulch
by his thick white collar. He's on show
like a clown. He drags a beige feather that he removed,
one time, from an old lady's hat.
We laugh and we touch.
I promise you love. Time will not take away that.

From the Garden

Come, my beloved,
consider the lilies.
We are of little faith.
We talk too much.
Put your mouthful of words away
and come with me to watch
the lilies open in such a field,
growing there like yachts,
slowly steering their petals
without nurses or clocks.
Let us consider the view:
a house where white clouds
decorate the muddy halls.
Oh, put away your good words
and your bad words. Spit out
your words like stones!
Come here! Come here!
Come eat my pleasant fruits.

Old

I'm afraid of needles
I'm tired of rubber sheets and tubes.
I'm tired of faces that I don't know
and now I think that death is starting.
Death starts like a dream,
full of objects and my sister's laughter.
We are young and we are walking
and picking wild blueberries
all the way to Damariscotta.
Oh Susan, she cried,
you've stained your new waist.
Sweet taste –
my mouth so full
and the sweet blue running out
all the way to Damariscotta.
What are you doing? Leave me alone!
Can't you see I'm dreaming?
In a dream you are never eighty.

from Doors, Doors, Doors

1. Old Man

Old man, it's four flights up and for what?
Your room is hardly any bigger than your bed.
Puffing as you climb, you are a brown woodcut
stooped over the thin rail and the wornout tread.

The room will do. All that's left of the old life
is jampacked on shelves from floor to ceiling
like a supermarket: your books, your dead wife
generously fat in her polished frame, the congealing

bowl of cornflakes sagging in their instant milk,
your hot plate and your one luxury, a telephone.
You leave your door open, lounging in maroon silk
and smiling at the other roomers who live alone.
Well, almost alone. Through the old-fashioned wall
the fellow next door has a girl who comes to call.

Twice a week at noon during their lunch hour
they pause by your door to peer into your world.
They speak sadly as if the wine they carry would sour
or as if the mattress would not keep them curled

together, extravagantly young in their tight lock.
Old man, you are their father holding court
in the dingy hall until their alarm clock
rings and unwinds them. You unstopper the quart

of brandy you've saved, examining the small print
in the telephone book. The phone in your lap is all
that's left of your family name. Like a Romanoff prince
you stay the same in your small alcove off the hall.
Castaway, your time is a flat sea that doesn't stop,
with no new land to make for and no new stories to swap.

The Black Art

A woman who writes feels too much,
those trances and portents!
As if cycles and children and islands
weren't enough; as if mourners and gossips
and vegetables were never enough.
She thinks she can warn the stars.
A writer is essentially a spy.
Dear love, I am that girl.

A man who writes knows too much,
such spells and fetiches!
As if erections and congresses and products
weren't enough; as if machines and galleons
and wars were never enough.
With used furniture he makes a tree.
A writer is essentially a crook.
Dear love, you are that man.

Never loving ourselves,
hating even our shoes and our hats,
we love each other, *precious, precious*.
Our hands are light blue and gentle.
Our eyes are full of terrible confessions.
But when we marry,
the children leave in disgust.
There is too much food and no one left over
to eat up all the weird abundance.

In the Deep Museum

My God, my God, what queer corner am I in?
Didn't I die, blood running down the post,
lungs gagging for air, die there for the sin
of anyone, my sour mouth giving up the ghost?
Surely my body is done? Surely I died?
And yet, I know, I'm here. What place is this?
Cold and queer, I sting with life. I lied.
Yes, I lied. Or else in some damned cowardice
my body would not give me up. I touch
fine cloth with my hands and my cheeks are cold.
If this is hell, then hell could not be much,
neither as special nor as ugly as I was told.

What's that I hear, snuffling and pawing its way
toward me? Its tongue knocks a pebble out of place
as it slides in, a sovereign. How can I pray?
It is panting; it is an odor with a face
like the skin of a donkey. It laps my sores.
It is hurt, I think, as I touch its little head.
It bleeds. I have forgiven murderers and whores
and now I must wait like old Jonah, not dead
nor alive, stroking a clumsy animal. A rat.
His teeth test me; he waits like a good cook,
knowing his own ground. I forgive him that,
as I forgave my Judas the money he took.

Now I hold his soft red sore to my lips
as his brothers crowd in, hairy angels who take
my gift. My ankles are a flute. I lose hips
and wrists. For three days, for love's sake,

I bless this other death. Oh, not in air –
in dirt. Under the rotting veins of its roots,
under the markets, under the sheep bed where
the hill is food, under the slippery fruits
of the vineyard, I go. Unto the bellies and jaws
of rats I commit my prophecy and fear.
Far below The Cross, I correct its flaws.
We have kept the miracle. I will not be here.

For Eleanor Boylan Talking with God

God has a brown voice,
as soft and full as beer.
Eleanor, who is more beautiful than my mother,
is standing in her kitchen talking
and I am breathing in my cigarettes like poison.
She stands in her lemon-colored sun dress
motioning to God with her wet hands
glossy from the washing of egg plates.
She tells him! She tells him like a drunk
who doesn't need to see to talk.
It's casual but friendly.
God is as close as the ceiling.

Though no one can ever know,
I don't think he has a face.
He had a face when I was six and a half.
Now he is large, covering up the sky
like a great resting jellyfish.
When I was eight I thought the dead people
stayed up there like blimps.
Now my chair is as hard as a scarecrow
and outside the summer flies sing like a choir.
Eleanor, before he leaves tell him . . .
Oh Eleanor, Eleanor,
tell him before death uses you up.

from *Live or Die*

(1966)

Flee On Your Donkey

Ma faim, Anne, Anne,
Fuis sur ton âne . . . Rimbaud

Because there was no other place
to flee to,
I came back to the scene of the disordered senses,
came back last night at midnight,
arriving in the thick June night
without luggage or defenses,
giving up my car keys and my cash,
keeping only a pack of Salem cigarettes
the way a child holds on to a toy.
I signed myself in where a stranger
puts the inked-in X's –
for this is a mental hospital,
not a child's game.

Today an interne knocks my knees,
testing for reflexes.
Once I would have winked and begged for dope.
Today I am terribly patient.
Today crows play black-jack
on the stethoscope.

Everyone has left me
except my muse,
that good nurse.
She stays in my hand,
a mild white mouse.

The curtains, lazy and delicate,
billow and flutter and drop
like the Victorian skirts
of my two maiden aunts
who kept an antique shop.

Hornets have been sent.
They cluster like floral arrangements on the screen.
Hornets, dragging their thin stingers,
hover outside, all knowing,
hissing: *the hornet knows.*
I heard it as a child
but what was it that he meant?
The hornet knows!
What happened to Jack and Doc and Reggy?

Who remembers what lurks in the heart of man?
What did The Green Hornet mean, *he knows?*
Or have I got it wrong?
Is it The Shadow who had seen
me from my beside radio?

Now it's *Dinn, Dinn, Dinn!*
while the ladies in the next room argue
and pick their teeth.
Upstairs a girl curls like a snail;
in another room someone tries to eat a shoe;
meanwhile an adolescent pads up and down
the hall in his white tennis socks.
A new doctor makes rounds
advertising tranquilizers, insulin, or shock
to the uninitiated.

Six years of such small preoccupations!
Six years of shuttling in and out of this place!
O my hunger! My hunger!

I could have gone around the world twice
or had new children – all boys.
It was a long trip with little days in it
and no new places.

In here,
it's the same old crowd,
the same ruined scene.
The alcoholic arrives with his golf clubs.
The suicide arrives with extra pills sewn
into the lining of her dress.
The permanent guests have done nothing new.
Their faces are still small
like babies with jaundice.

Meanwhile,
they carried out my mother,
wrapped like somebody's doll, in sheets,
bandaged her jaw and stuffed up her holes.
My father, too. He went out on the rotten blood
he used up on other women in the Middle West.
He went out, a cured old alcoholic
on crooked feet and useless hands.
He went out calling for his father
who died all by himself long ago –
that fat banker who got locked up,
his genes suspended like dollars,
wrapped up in his secret,
tied up securely in a straitjacket.

But you, my doctor, my enthusiast,
were better than Christ;
you promised me another world
to tell me who
I was.

I spent most of my time,
a stranger,
damned and in trance – that little hut,
that naked blue-veined place,
my eyes shut on the confusing office,
eyes circling into my childhood,
eyes newly cut.
Years of hints
strung out – a serialized case history –
thirty-three years of the same dull incest
that sustained us both.
You, my bachelor analyst,
who sat on Marlborough Street,
sharing your office with your mother
and giving up cigarettes each New Year,
were the new God,
the manager of the Gideon Bible.

I was your third-grader
with a blue star on my forehead.
In trance I could be any age,
voice, gesture – all turned backward
like a drugstore clock.
Awake, I memorized dreams.
Dreams came into the ring
like third string fighters,
each one a bad bet
who might win
because there was no other.

I stared at them,
concentrating on the abyss
the way one looks down into a rock quarry,
uncountable miles down,
my hands swinging down like hooks
to pull dreams up out of their cage.
O my hunger! My hunger!

Once,
outside your office,
I collapsed in the old-fashioned swoon
between the illegally parked cars.
I threw myself down,
pretending dead for eight hours.
I thought I had died
into a snowstorm.
Above my head
chains cracked along like teeth
digging their way through the snowy street.
I lay there
like an overcoat
that someone had thrown away.
You carried me back in,
awkwardly, tenderly,
with the help of the red-haired secretary
who was built like a lifeguard.
My shoes,
I remember,
were lost in the snowbank
as if I planned never to walk again.

That was the winter
that my mother died,
half mad on morphine,
blown up, at last,
like a pregnant pig.
I was her dreamy evil eye.
In fact,
I carried a knife in my pocketbook –
my husband's good L. L. Bean hunting knife.
I wasn't sure if I should slash a tire
or scrape the guts out of some dream.

You taught me
to believe in dreams;
thus I was the dredger.
I held them like an old woman with arthritic fingers,
carefully straining the water out –
sweet dark playthings,
and above all, mysterious
until they grew mournful and weak.
O my hunger! My hunger!
I was the one
who opened the warm eyelid
like a surgeon
and brought forth young girls
to grunt like fish.

I told you,
I said –
but I was lying –
that the knife was for my mother . . .
and then I delivered her.

The curtains flutter out
and slump against the bars.
They are my two thin ladies
named Blanche and Rose.
The grounds outside
are pruned like an estate at Newport.
Far off, in the field,
something yellow grows.

Was it last month or last year
that the ambulance ran like a hearse
with its siren blowing on suicide –
Dinn, dinn, dinn! –
a noon whistle that kept insisting on life
all the way through the traffic lights?

I have come back
but disorder is not what it was.
I have lost the trick of it!
The innocence of it!
That fellow-patient in his stovepipe hat
with his fiery joke, his manic smile –
even he seems blurred, small and pale.
I have come back,
recommitted,
fastened to the wall like a bathroom plunger,
held like a prisoner
who was so poor
he fell in love with jail.

I stand at this old window
complaining of the soup,
examining the grounds,
allowing myself the wasted life.
Soon I will raise my face for a white flag,
and when God enters the fort,
I won't spit or gag on his finger.
I will eat it like a white flower.
Is this the old trick, the wasting away,
the skull that waits for its dose
of electric power?

This is madness
but a kind of hunger.
What good are my questions
in this hierarchy of death
where the earth and the stones go
Dinn! Dinn! Dinn!
It is hardly a feast.
It is my stomach that makes me suffer.

Turn, my hungers!
For once make a deliberate decision.
There are brains that rot here
like black bananas.
Hearts have grown as flat as dinner plates.
Anne, Anne,
flee on your donkey,
flee this sad hotel,
ride out on some hairy beast,
gallop backward pressing
your buttocks to his withers,
sit to his clumsy gait somehow.
Ride out
any old way you please!
In this place everyone talks to his own mouth.
That's what it means to be crazy.
Those I loved best died of it –
the fool's disease.

Consorting with Angels

I was tired of being a woman,
tired of the spoons and the pots,
tired of my mouth and my breasts,
tired of the cosmetics and the silks.
There were still men who sat at my table,
circled around the bowl I offered up.
The bowl was filled with purple grapes
and the flies hovered in for the scent
and even my father came with his white bone.
But I was tired of the gender of things.

Last night I had a dream
and I said to it . . .
'You are the answer.
You will outlive my husband and my father.'
In that dream there was a city made of chains
where Joan was put to death in man's clothes
and the nature of the angels went unexplained,
no two made in the same species,
one with a nose, one with an ear in its hand,
one chewing a star and recording its orbit,
each one like a poem obeying itself,
performing God's functions,
a people apart.

'You are the answer,'
I said, and entered,
lying down on the gates of the city.
Then the chains were fastened around me
and I lost my common gender and my final aspect.

Adam was on the left of me
and Eve was on the right of me,
both thoroughly inconsistent with the world of reason.
We wove our arms together
and rode under the sun.
I was not a woman anymore,
not one thing or the other.

O daughter of Jerusalem,
the king has brought me into his chamber.
I am black and I am beautiful.
I've been opened and undressed.
I have no arms or legs.
I'm all one skin like a fish.
I'm no more a woman
than Christ was a man.

Love Song

I was
the girl of the chain letter,
the girl full of talk of coffins and keyholes,
the one of the telephone bills,
the wrinkled photo and the lost connections,
the one who kept saying –
Listen! Listen!
We must never! We must never!
and all those things . . .

the one
with her eyes half under her coat,
with her large gun-metal blue eyes,
with the thin vein at the bend of her neck
that hummed like a tuning fork,
with her shoulders as bare as a building,
with her thin foot and her thin toes,
with an old red hook in her mouth,
the mouth that kept bleeding
into the terrible fields of her soul . . .

the one
who kept dropping off to sleep,
as old as a stone she was,
each hand like a piece of cement,
for hours and hours
and then she'd wake,
after the small death,
and then she'd be as soft as,
as delicate as . . .

as soft and delicate as
an excess of light,
with nothing dangerous at all,
like a beggar who eats
or a mouse on a rooftop
with no trap doors,
with nothing more honest
than your hand in her hand –
with nobody, nobody but you!
and all those things.
nobody, nobody but you!
Oh! There is no translating
that ocean,
that music,
that theater,
that field of ponies.

Sylvia's Death

for Sylvia Plath

O Sylvia, Sylvia,
with a dead box of stones and spoons,

with two children, two meteors
wandering loose in the tiny playroom,

with your mouth into the sheet,
into the roofbeam, into the dumb prayer,

(Sylvia, Sylvia,
where did you go
after you wrote me
from Devonshire
about raising potatoes
and keeping bees?)

what did you stand by,
just how did you lie down into?

Thief! –
how did you crawl into,

crawl down alone
into the death I wanted so badly and for so long,

the death we said we both outgrew,
the one we wore on our skinny breasts,

the one we talked of so often each time
we downed three extra dry martinis in Boston,

the death that talked of analysts and cures,
the death that talked like brides with plots,

the death we drank to,
the motives and then the quiet deed?

(In Boston
the dying
ride in cabs,
yes death again,
that ride home
with *our* boy.)

O Sylvia, I remember the sleepy drummer
who beat on our eyes with an old story,

how we wanted to let him come
like a sadist or a New York fairy

to do his job,
a necessity, a window in a wall or a crib,

and since that time he waited
under our heart, our cupboard,

and I see now that we store him up
year after year, old suicides

and I know at the news of your death,
a terrible taste for it, like salt.

(And me,
me too.
And now, Sylvia,
you again
with death again,
that ride home
with *our* boy.)

And I say only
with my arms stretched out into that stone place,

what is your death
but an old belonging,

a mole that fell out
of one of your poems?

(O friend,
while the moon's bad,
and the king's gone,
and the queen's at her wit's end
the bar fly ought to sing!)

O tiny mother,
you too!
O funny duchess!
O blonde thing!

Protestant Easter

eight years old

When he was a little boy
Jesus was good all the time.
No wonder that he grew up to be such a big shot
who could forgive people so much.
When he died everyone was mean.
Later on he rose when no one else was looking.
Either he was hiding or else
he went up.
Maybe he was only hiding?
Maybe he could fly?

Yesterday I found a purple crocus
blowing its way out of the snow.
It was all alone.
It was getting its work done.
Maybe Jesus was only getting his work done
and letting God blow him off the Cross
and maybe he was afraid for a minute
so he hid under the big stones.
He was smart to go to sleep up there
even though his mother got so sad
and let them put him in a cave.
I sat in a tunnel when I was five.
That tunnel, my mother said,
went straight into the big river
and so I never went again.
Maybe Jesus knew my tunnel
and crawled right through to the river
so he could wash all the blood off.

Maybe he only meant to get clean
and then come back again?
Don't tell me that he went up in smoke
like Daddy's cigar!
He didn't blow out like a match!

It is special
being here at Easter
with the Cross they built like a capital T.
The ceiling is an upside-down rowboat.
I usually count its ribs.
Maybe he was drowning?
Or maybe we are all upside down?
I can see the face of a mouse inside
of all that stained-glass window.
Well, it could be a mouse!
Once I thought the Bunny Rabbit was special
and I hunted for eggs.
That's when I was seven.
I'm grownup now. Now it's really Jesus.
I just have to get Him straight.
And right now.

Who are we anyhow?
What do we belong to?
Are we a *we*?
I think that he rose
but I'm not quite sure
and they don't really say
singing their *Alleluia*
in the churchy way.
Jesus was on that Cross.
After that they pounded nails into his hands.
After that, well, after that,
everyone wore hats
and then there was a big stone rolled away

and then almost everyone –
the ones who sit up straight –
looked at the ceiling.

Alleluia they sing.
They don't know.
They don't care if he was hiding or flying.
Well, it doesn't matter how he got there.
It matters where he was going.
The important thing for me
is that I'm wearing white gloves.
I always sit straight,
I keep on looking at the ceiling.
And about Jesus,
they couldn't be sure of it,
not so sure of it anyhow,
so they decided to become Protestants.
Those are the people that sing
when they aren't quite
sure.

Menstruation at Forty

I was thinking of a son.
The womb is not a clock
nor a bell tolling,
but in the eleventh month of its life
I feel the November
of the body as well as of the calendar.
In two days it will be my birthday
and as always the earth is done with its harvest.
This time I hunt for death,
the night I lean toward,
the night I want.
Well then –
speak of it!
It was in the womb all along.

I was thinking of a son . . .
You! The never acquired,
the never seeded or unfastened,
you of the genitals I feared,
the stalk and the puppy's breath.
Will I give you my eyes or his?
Will you be the David or the Susan?
(Those two names I picked and listened for.)
Can you be the man your fathers are –
the leg muscles from Michelangelo,
hands from Yugoslavia,
somewhere the peasant, Slavic and determined,
somewhere the survivor, bulging with life –
and could it still be possible,
all this with Susan's eyes?

All this without you –
two days gone in blood.
I myself will die without baptism,
a third daughter they didn't bother.
My death will come on my name day.
What's wrong with the name day?
It's only an angel of the sun.
Woman,
weaving a web over your own,
a thin and tangled poison.
Scorpio,
bad spider –
die!

My death from the wrists,
two name tags,
blood worn like a corsage
to bloom
one on the left and one on the right –
It's a warm room,
the place of the blood.
Leave the door open on its hinges!

Two days for your death
and two days until mine.

Love! That red disease –
year after year, David, you would make me wild!
David! Susan! David! David!
full and disheveled, hissing into the night,
never growing old,
waiting always for you on the porch . . .
year after year,
my carrot, my cabbage,
I would have possessed you before all women,
calling your name,
calling you mine.

Wanting to Die

Since you ask, most days I cannot remember.
I walk in my clothing, unmarked by that voyage.
Then the almost unnameable lust returns.

Even then I have nothing against life.
I know well the grass blades you mention,
the furniture you have placed under the sun.

But suicides have a special language.
Like carpenters they want to know *which tools*.
They never ask *why build*.

Twice I have so simply declared myself,
have possessed the enemy, eaten the enemy,
have taken on his craft, his magic.

In this way, heavy and thoughtful,
warmer than oil or water,
I have rested, drooling at the mouth-hole.

I did not think of my body at needle point.
Even the cornea and the leftover urine were gone.
Suicides have already betrayed the body.

Still-born, they don't always die,
but dazzled, they can't forget a drug so sweet
that even children would look on and smile.

To thrust all that life under your tongue! –
that, all by itself, becomes a passion.
Death's a sad bone; bruised, you'd say,

and yet she waits for me, year after year,
to so delicately undo an old wound,
to empty my breath from its bad prison.

Balanced there, suicides sometimes meet,
raging at the fruit, a pumped-up moon,
leaving the bread they mistook for a kiss,

leaving the page of the book carelessly open,
something unsaid, the phone off the hook
and the love, whatever it was, an infection.

Little Girl, My String Bean, My Lovely Woman

My daughter, at eleven
(almost twelve), is like a garden.

Oh, darling! Born in that sweet birthday suit
and having owned it and known it for so long,
now you must watch high noon enter –
noon, that ghost hour.
Oh, funny little girl – this one under a blueberry sky,
this one! How can I say that I've known
just what you know and just where you are?

It's not a strange place, this odd home
where your face sits in my hand
so full of distance,
so full of its immediate fever.
The summer has seized you,
as when, last month in Amalfi, I saw
lemons as large as your desk-side globe –
that miniature map of the world –
and I could mention, too,
the market stalls of mushrooms
and garlic buds all engorged.
Or I think even of the orchard next door,
where the berries are done
and the apples are beginning to swell.
And once, with our first backyard,
I remember I planted an acre of yellow beans
we couldn't eat.

Oh, little girl,
my stringbean,
how do you grow?
You grow this way.
You are too many to eat.

I hear
as in a dream
the conversation of the old wives
speaking of *womanhood.*
I remember that I heard nothing myself.
I was alone.
I waited like a target.

Let high noon enter –
the hour of the ghosts.
Once the Romans believed
that noon was the ghost hour,
and I can believe it, too,
under that startling sun,
and someday they will come to you,
someday, men bare to the waist, young Romans
at noon where they belong,
with ladders and hammers
while no one sleeps.

But before they enter
I will have said,
Your bones are lovely,
and before their strange hands
there was always this hand that formed.

Oh, darling, let your body in,
let it tie you in,
in comfort.
What I want to say, Linda,
is that women are born twice.

If I could have watched you grow
as a magical mother might,
if I could have seen through my magical transparent belly,
there would have been such ripening within:
your embryo,
the seed taking on its own,
life clapping the bedpost,
bones from the pond,
thumbs and two mysterious eyes,
the awfully human head,
the heart jumping like a puppy,
the important lungs,
the becoming –
while it becomes!
as it does now,
a world of its own,
a delicate place.

I say hello
to such shakes and knockings and high jinks,
such music, such sprouts,
such dancing-mad-bears of music,
such necessary sugar,
such goings-on!

Oh, little girl,
my stringbean,
how do you grow?
You grow this way.
You are too many to eat.

What I want to say, Linda,
is that there is nothing in your body that lies.
All that is new is telling the truth.
I'm here, that somebody else,
an old tree in the background.

Darling,
stand still at your door,
sure of yourself, a white stone, a good stone –
as exceptional as laughter
you will strike fire,
that new thing!

Suicide Note

You speak to me of narcissism but I reply that it is a matter of my life . . . Artaud

At this time let me somehow bequeath all the leftovers to my daughters and their daughters . . . Anonymous

Better,
despite the worms talking to
the mare's hoof in the field;
better,
despite the season of young girls
dropping their blood;
better somehow
to drop myself quickly
into an old room.
Better (someone said)
not to be born
and far better
not to be born twice
at thirteen
where the boardinghouse,
each year a bedroom,
caught fire.

Dear friend,
I will have to sink with hundreds of others
on a dumbwaiter into hell.
I will be a light thing.
I will enter death
like someone's lost optical lens.
Life is half enlarged.

The fish and owls are fierce today.
Life tilts backward and forward.
Even the wasps cannot find my eyes.

Yes,
eyes that were immediate once.
Eyes that have been truly awake,
eyes that told the whole story –
poor dumb animals.
Eyes that were pierced,
little nail heads,
light blue gunshots.

And once with
a mouth like a cup,
clay colored or blood colored,
open like the breakwater
for the lost ocean
and open like the noose
for the first head.

Once upon a time
my hunger was for Jesus.
O my hunger! My hunger!
Before he grew old
he rode calmly into Jerusalem
in search of death.

This time
I certainly
do not ask for understanding
and yet I hope everyone else
will turn their heads when an unrehearsed fish jumps
on the surface of Echo Lake;
when moonlight,
its bass note turned up loud,

hurts some building in Boston,
when the truly beautiful lie together.
I think of this, surely,
and would think of it far longer
if I were not . . . if I were not
at that old fire.

I could admit
that I am only a coward
crying *me me me*
and not mention the little gnats, the moths,
forced by circumstance
to suck on the electric bulb.
But surely you know that everyone has a death,
his own death,
waiting for him.
So I will go now
without old age or disease,
wildly but accurately,
knowing my best route,
carried by that toy donkey I rode all these years,
never asking, 'Where are we going?'
We were riding (if I'd only known)
to this.

Dear friend,
please do not think
that I visualize guitars playing
or my father arching his bone.
I do not even expect my mother's mouth.
I know that I have died before –
once in November, once in June.
How strange to choose June again,
so concrete with its green breasts and bellies.
Of course guitars will not play!
The snakes will certainly not notice.

New York City will not mind.
At night the bats will beat on the trees,
knowing it all,
seeing what they sensed all the day.

Pain for a Daughter

Blind with love, my daughter
has cried nightly for horses,
those long-necked marchers and churners
that she has mastered, any and all,
reigning them in like a circus hand –
the excitable muscles and the ripe neck;
tending this summer, a pony and a foal.
She who is too squeamish to pull
a thorn from the dog's paw,
watched her pony blossom with distemper,
the underside of the jaw swelling
like an enormous grape.
Gritting her teeth with love,
she drained the boil and scoured it
with hydrogen peroxide until pus
ran like milk on the barn floor.

Blind with loss all winter,
in dungarees, a ski jacket and a hard hat,
she visits the neighbor's stable,
our acreage not zoned for barns;
they who own the flaming horses
and the swan-whipped thoroughbred
that she tugs at and cajoles,
thinking it will burn like a furnace
under her small-hipped English seat.

Blind with pain she limps home.
The thoroughbred has stood on her foot.
He rested there like a building.

He grew into her foot until they were one.
The marks of the horseshoe printed
into her flesh, the tips of her toes
ripped off like pieces of leather,
three toenails swirled like shells
and left to float in blood in her riding boot.

Blind with fear, she sits on the toilet,
her foot balanced over the washbasin,
her father, hydrogen peroxide in hand,
performing the rites of the cleansing.
She bites on a towel, sucked in breath,
sucked in and arched against the pain,
her eyes glancing off me where
I stand at the door, eyes locked
on the ceiling, eyes of a stranger,
and then she cries . . .
Oh my God, help me!
Where a child would have cried *Mama!*
Where a child would have believed *Mama!*
she bit the towel and called on God
and I saw her life stretch out . . .
I saw her torn in childbirth,
and I saw her, at that moment,
in her own death and I knew that she
knew.

The Addict

Sleepmonger,
deathmonger,
with capsules in my-palms each night,
eight at a time from sweet pharmaceutical bottles
I make arrangements for a pint-sized journey.
I'm the queen of this condition.
I'm an expert on making the trip
and now they say I'm an addict.
Now they ask why.
Why!

Don't they know
that I promised to die!
I'm keeping in practice.
I'm merely staying in shape.
The pills are a mother, but better,
every color and as good as sour balls.
I'm on a diet from death.

Yes, I admit
it has gotten to be a bit of a habit –
blows eight at a time, socked in the eye,
hauled away by the pink, the orange,
the green and the white goodnights.
I'm becoming something of a chemical
mixture.
That's it!

My supply
of tablets

has got to last for years and years.
I like them more than I like me.
Stubborn as hell, they won't let go.
It's a kind of marriage.
It's a kind of war
where I plant bombs inside
of myself.

Yes
I try
to kill myself in small amounts,
an innocuous occupation.
Actually I'm hung up on it.
But remember I don't make too much noise.
And frankly no one has to lug me out
and I don't stand there in my winding sheet.
I'm a little buttercup in my yellow nightie
eating my eight loaves in a row
and in a certain order as in
the laying on of hands
or the black sacrament.

It's a ceremony
but like any other sport
it's full of rules.
It's like a musical tennis match where
my mouth keeps catching the ball.
Then I lie on my altar
elevated by the eight chemical kisses.

What a lay me down this is
with two pink, two orange,
two green, two white goodnights.
Fee-fi-fo-fum –
Now I'm borrowed.
Now I'm numb.

Cripples and Other Stories

My doctor, the comedian
I called you every time
and made you laugh yourself
when I wrote this silly rhyme . . .

> Each time I give lectures
> or gather in the grants
> you send me off to boarding school
> in training pants.

God damn it, father-doctor.
I'm really thirty-six.
I see dead rats in the toilet.
I'm one of the lunatics.

Disgusted, mother put me
on the potty. She was good at this.
My father was fat on scotch.
It leaked from every orifice.

Oh the enemas of childhood,
reeking of outhouses and shame!
Yet you rock me in your arms
and whisper my nickname.

Or else you hold my hand
and teach me love too late.
And that's the hand of the arm
they tried to amputate.

Though I was almost seven
I was an awful brat.
I put it in the Easy Wringer.
It came out nice and flat.

It was an instant cripple
from my finger to my shoulder.
The laundress wept and swooned.
My mother had to hold her.

I knew I was a cripple
Of course, I'd known it from the start.
My father took the crowbar
and broke that wringer's heart.

The surgeons shook their heads.
They really didn't know –
Would the cripple inside of me
be a cripple that would show?

My father was a perfect man,
clean and rich and fat.
My mother was a brilliant thing.
She was good at that.

You hold me in your arms.
How strange that you're so tender!
Child-woman that I am,
you think that you can mend her.

As for the arm,
unfortunately it grew.
Though mother said a withered arm
would put me in *Who's Who*.

For years she described it.
She sang it like a hymn.
By then she loved the shrunken thing,
my little withered limb.

My father's cells clicked each night,
intent on making money.
And as for my cells, they brooded,
little queens, on honey.

On boys too, as a matter of fact,
and cigarettes and cars.
Mother frowned at my wasted life.
My father smoked cigars.

My cheeks blossomed with maggots.
I picked at them like pearls.
I covered them with pancake.
I wound my hair in curls.

My father didn't know me
but you kiss me in my fever.
My mother knew me twice
and then I had to leave her.

But those are just two stories
and I have more to tell
from the outhouse, the greenhouse
where you draw me out of hell.

Father, I'm thirty-six,
yet I lie here in your crib.
I'm getting born again, Adam,
as you prod me with your rib.

Live

Live or die, but don't poison everything . . .

Well, death's been here
for a long time –
it has a hell of a lot
to do with hell
and suspicion of the eye
and the religious objects
and how I mourned them
when they were made obscene
by my dwarf-heart's doodle.
The chief ingredient
is mutilation.
And mud, day after day,
mud like a ritual,
and the baby on the platter,
cooked but still human,
cooked also with little maggots,
sewn onto it maybe by somebody's mother,
the damn bitch!

Even so,
I kept right on going on,
a sort of human statement,
lugging myself as if
I were a sawed-off body
in the trunk, the steamer trunk.
This became a perjury of the soul.
It became an outright lie
and even though I dressed the body
it was still naked, still killed.

It was caught
in the first place at birth,
like a fish.
But I played it, dressed it up,
dressed it up like somebody's doll.

Is life something you play?
And all the time wanting to get rid of it?
And further, everyone yelling at you
to shut up. And no wonder!
People don't like to be told
that you're sick
and then be forced
to watch
you
come
down with the hammer.

Today life opened inside me like an egg
and there inside
after considerable digging
I found the answer.
What a bargain!
There was the sun,
her yolk moving feverishly,
tumbling her prize –
and you realize that she does this daily!
I'd known she was a purifier
but I hadn't thought
she was solid,
hadn't known she was an answer.
God! It's a dream,
lovers sprouting in the yard
like celery stalks
and better,
a husband straight as a redwood,

two daughters, two sea urchins,
picking roses off my hackles.
If I'm on fire they dance around it
and cook marshmallows.
And if I'm ice
they simply skate on me
in little ballet costumes.

Here,
all along,
thinking I was a killer,
anointing myself daily
with my little poisons.
But no.
I'm an empress.
I wear an apron.
My typewriter writes.
It didn't break the way it warned.
Even crazy, I'm as nice
as a chocolate bar.
Even with the witches' gymnastics
they trust my incalculable city,
my corruptible bed.

O dearest three,
I make a soft reply.
The witch comes on
and you paint her pink.
I come with kisses in my hood
and the sun, the smart one,
rolling in my arms.
So I say Live
and turn my shadow three times round
to feed our puppies as they come,
the eight Dalmatians we didn't drown,
despite the warnings: The abort! The destroy!

Despite the pails of water that waited
to drown them, to pull them down like stones,
they came, each one headfirst,
blowing bubbles the color of cataract-blue
and fumbling for the tiny tits.
Just last week, eight Dalmatians,
¾ of a lb., lined up like cord wood
each
like a
birch tree.
I promise to love more if they come,
because in spite of cruelty
and the stuffed railroad cars for the ovens,
I am not what I expected. Not an Eichmann.
The poison just didn't take.
So I won't hang around in my hospital shift,
repeating The Black Mass and all of it.
I say *Live, Live* because of the sun,
the dream, the excitable gift.

from *Love Poems*

(1969)

The Interrogation of the Man of Many Hearts

Who's she,
that one in your arms?

She's the one I carried my bones to
and built a house that was just a cot
and built a life that was over an hour
and built a castle where no one lives
and built, in the end, a song
to go with the ceremony.

Why have you brought her here?
Why do you knock on my door
with your little stories and songs?

I had joined her the way a man joins
a woman and yet there was no place
for festivities or formalities
and these things matter to a woman
and, you see, we live in a cold climate
and are not permitted to kiss on the street
so I made up a song that wasn't true.
I made up a song called *Marriage*.

You come to me out of wedlock
and kick your foot on my stoop
and ask me to measure such things?

Never. Never. Not my real wife.
She's my real witch, my fork, my mare,
my mother of tears, my skirtful of hell,

the stamp of my sorrows, the stamp of my bruises
and also the children she might bear
and also a private place, a body of bones
that I would honestly buy, if I could buy,
that I would marry, if I could marry.

And should I torment you for that?
Each man has a small fate allotted to him
and yours is a passionate one.

But I am in torment. We have no place.
The cot we share is almost a prison
where I can't say buttercup, bobolink,
sugarduck, pumpkin, love ribbon, locket,
valentine, summergirl, funnygirl and all
those nonsense things one says in bed.
To say I have bedded with her is not enough.
I have not only bedded her down.
I have tied her down with a knot.

Then why do you stick your fists
into your pockets? Why do you shuffle
your feet like a schoolboy?

For years I have tied this knot in my dreams.
I have walked through a door in my dreams
and she was standing there in my mother's apron.
Once she crawled through a window that was shaped
like a keyhole and she was wearing my daughter's
pink corduroys and each time I tied these women
in a knot. Once a queen came. I tied her too.
But this is something I have actually tied
and now I have made her fast.
I sang her out. I caught her down.
I stamped her out with a song.
There was no other apartment for it.

There was no other chamber for it.
Only the knot. The bedded-down knot.
Thus I have laid my hands upon her
and have called her eyes and her mouth
as mine, and also her tongue.

Why do you ask me to make choices?
I am not a judge or a psychologist.
You own your bedded-down knot.

And yet I have real daytimes and nighttimes
with children and balconies and a good wife.
Thus I have tied these other knots,
yet I would rather not think of them
when I speak to you of her. Not now.
If she were a room to rent I would pay.
If she were a life to save I would save.
Maybe I am a man of many hearts.

A man of many hearts?
Why then do you tremble at my doorway?
A man of many hearts does not need me.

I'm caught deep in the dye of her.
I have allowed you to catch me red-handed,
catch me with my wild oats in a wild clock
for my mare, my dove and my own clean body.
People might say I have snakes in my boots
but I tell you that just once am I in the stirrups,
just once, this once, in the cup.
The love of the woman is in the song.
I called her the woman in red.
I called her the girl in pink
but she was ten colors
and ten women.
I could hardly name her.

I know who she is.
You have named her enough.

Maybe I shouldn't have put it in words.
Frankly, I think I'm worse for this kissing,
drunk as a piper, kicking the traces
and determined to tie her up forever.
You see the song is the life,
the life I can't live.
God, even as he passes,
hands down monogamy like slang.
I wanted to write her into the law.
But, you know, there is no law for this.

Man of many hearts, you are a fooll
The clover has grown thorns this year
and robbed the cattle of their fruit
and the stones of the river
have sucked men's eyes dry,
season after season,
and every bed has been condemned,
not by morality or law,
but by time.

In Celebration of My Uterus

Everyone in me is a bird.
I am beating all my wings.
They wanted to cut you out
but they will not.
They said you were immeasurably empty
but you are not.
They said you were sick unto dying
but they were wrong.
You are singing like a school girl.
You are not torn.

Sweet weight,
in celebration of the woman I am
and of the soul of the woman I am
and of the central creature and its delight
I sing for you. I dare to live.
Hello, spirit. Hello, cup.
Fasten, cover. Cover that does contain.
Hello to the soil of the fields.
Welcome, roots.

Each cell has a life.
There is enough here to please a nation.
It is enough that the populace own these goods.
Any person, any commonwealth would say of it,
'It is good this year that we may plant again
and think forward to a harvest.
A blight had been forecast and has been cast out.'
Many women are singing together of this:
one is in a shoe factory cursing the machine,

one is at the aquarium tending a seal,
one is dull at the wheel of her Ford,
one is at the toll gate collecting,
one is tying the cord of a calf in Arizona,
one is straddling a cello in Russia,
one is shifting pots on the stove in Egypt,
one is painting her bedroom walls moon color,
one is dying but remembering a breakfast,
one is stretching on her mat in Thailand,
one is wiping the ass of her child,
one is staring out the window of a train
in the middle of Wyoming and one is
anywhere and some are everywhere and all
seem to be singing, although some can not
sing a note.

Sweet weight,
in celebration of the woman I am
let me carry a ten-foot scarf,
let me drum for the nineteen-year-olds,
let me carry bowls for the offering
(if that is my part).
Let me study the cardiovascular tissue,
let me examine the angular distance of meteors,
let me suck on the stems of flowers
(if that is my part).
Let me make certain tribal figures
(if that is my part).
For this thing the body needs
let me sing
for the supper,
for the kissing,
for the correct
yes.

For My Lover, Returning to His Wife

She is all there.
She was melted carefully down for you
and cast up from your childhood,
cast up from your one hundred favorite aggies.

She has always been there, my darling.
She is, in fact, exquisite.
Fireworks in the dull middle of February
and as real as a cast-iron pot.

Let's face it, I have been momentary.
A luxury. A bright red sloop in the harbor.
My hair rising like smoke from the car window.
Littleneck clams out of season.

She is more than that. She is your have to have,
has grown you your practical your tropical growth.
This is not an experiment. She is all harmony.
She sees to oars and oarlocks for the dinghy,

has placed wild flowers at the window at breakfast,
sat by the potter's wheel at midday,
set forth three children under the moon,
three cherubs drawn by Michelangelo,

done this with her legs spread out
in the terrible months in the chapel.
If you glance up, the children are there
like delicate balloons resting on the ceiling.

She has also carried each one down the hall
after supper, their heads privately bent,
two legs protesting, person to person,
her face flushed with a song and their little sleep.

I give you back your heart.
I give you permission –

for the fuse inside her, throbbing
angrily in the dirt, for the bitch in her
and the burying of her wound –
for the burying of her small red wound alive –

for the pale flickering flare under her ribs,
for the drunken sailor who waits in her left pulse,
for the mother's knee, for the stockings,
for the garter belt, for the call –

the curious call
when you will burrow in arms and breasts
and tug at the orange ribbon in her hair
and answer the call, the curious call.

She is so naked and singular.
She is the sum of yourself and your dream.
Climb her like a monument, step after step.
She is solid.

As for me, I am a watercolor.
I wash off.

It Is a Spring Afternoon

Everything here is yellow and green.
Listen to its throat, its earthskin,
the bone dry voices of the peepers
as they throb like advertisements.
The small animals of the woods
are carrying their deathmasks
into a narrow winter cave.
The scarecrow has plucked out
his two eyes like diamonds
and walked into the village.
The general and the postman
have taken off their packs.
This has all happened before
but nothing here is obsolete.
Everything here is possible.

Because of this
perhaps a young girl has laid down
her winter clothes and has casually
placed herself upon a tree limb
that hangs over a pool in the river.
She has been poured out onto the limb,
low above the houses of the fishes
as they swim in and out of her reflection
and up and down the stairs of her legs.
Her body carries clouds all the way home.
She is overlooking her watery face
in the river where blind men
come to bathe at midday.

Because of this
the ground, that winter nightmare,
has cured its sores and burst
with green birds and vitamins.
Because of this
the trees turn in their trenches
and hold up little rain cups
by their slender fingers.
Because of this
a woman stands by her stove
singing and cooking flowers.
Everything here is yellow and green.

Surely spring will allow
a girl without a stitch on
to turn softly in her sunlight
and not be afraid of her bed.
She has already counted seven
blossoms in her green green mirror.
Two rivers combine beneath her.
The face of the child wrinkles
in the water and is gone forever.
The woman is all that can be seen
in her animal loveliness.
Her cherished and obstinate skin
lies deeply under the watery tree.
Everything is altogether possible
and the blind men can also see.

Just Once

Just once I knew what life was for.
In Boston, quite suddenly, I understood;
walked there along the Charles River,
watched the lights copying themselves,
all neoned and strobe-hearted, opening
their mouths as wide as opera singers;
counted the stars, my little campaigners,
my scar daisies, and knew that I walked my love
on the night green side of it and cried
my heart to the eastbound cars and cried
my heart to the westbound cars and took
my truth across a small humped bridge
and hurried my truth, the charm of it, home
and hoarded these constants into morning
only to find them gone.

You All Know the Story of the Other Woman

It's a little Walden.
She is private in her breathbed
as his body takes off and flies,
flies straight as an arrow.
But it's a bad translation.
Daylight is nobody's friend.
God comes in like a landlord
and flashes on his brassy lamp.
Now she is just so-so.
He puts his bones back on,
turning the clock back an hour.
She knows flesh, that skin balloon,
the unbound limbs, the boards,
the roof, the removable roof.
She is his selection, part time.
You know the story too! Look,
when it is over he places her,
like a phone, back on the hook.

The Ballad of the Lonely Masturbator

The end of the affair is always death.
She's my workshop. Slippery eye,
out of the tribe of myself my breath
finds you gone. I horrify
those who stand by. I am fed.
At night, alone, I marry the bed.

Finger to finger, now she's mine.
She's not too far. She's my encounter.
I beat her like a bell. I recline
in the bower where you used to mount her.
You borrowed me on the flowered spread.
At night, alone, I marry the bed.

Take for instance this night, my love,
that every single couple puts together
with a joint overturning, beneath, above,
the abundant two on sponge and feather,
kneeling and pushing, head to head.
At night alone, I marry the bed.

I break out of my body this way,
an annoying miracle. Could I
put the dream market on display?
I am spread out. I crucify.
My little plum is what you said.
At night, alone, I marry the bed.

Then my black-eyed rival came.
The lady of water, rising on the beach,

a piano at her fingertips, shame
on her lips and a flute's speech.
And I was the knock-kneed broom instead.
At night, alone, I marry the bed.

She took you the way a woman takes
a bargain dress off the rack
and I broke the way a stone breaks.
I give back your books and fishing tack.
Today's paper says that you are wed.
At night, alone, I marry the bed.

The boys and girls are one tonight.
They unbutton blouses. They unzip flies.
They take off shoes. They turn off the light.
The glimmering creatures are full of lies.
They are eating each other. They are overfed.
At night, alone, I marry the bed.

Us

I was wrapped in black
fur and white fur and
you undid me and then
you placed me in gold light
and then you crowned me,
while snow fell outside
the door in diagonal darts.
While a ten-inch snow
came down like stars
in small calcium fragments,
we were in our own bodies
(that room that will bury us)
and you were in my body
(that room that will outlive us)
and at first I rubbed your
feet dry with a towel
because I was your slave
and then you called me princess.
Princess!

Oh then
I stood up in my gold skin
and I beat down the psalms
and I beat down the clothes
and you undid the bridle
and you undid the reins
and I undid the buttons,
the bones, the confusions,
the New England postcards,
the January ten o'clock night,

and we rose up like wheat,
acre after acre of gold,
and we harvested,
we harvested.

Mr. Mine

Notice how he has numbered the blue veins
in my breast. Moreover there are ten freckles.
Now he goes left. Now he goes right.
He is building a city, a city of flesh.
He's an industrialist. He has starved in cellars
and, ladies and gentlemen, he's been broken by iron,
by the blood, by the metal, by the triumphant
iron of his mother's death. But he begins again.
Now he constructs me. He is consumed by the city.
From the glory of boards he has built me up.
From the wonder of concrete he has molded me.
He has given me six hundred street signs.
The time I was dancing he built a museum.
He built ten blocks when I moved on the bed.
He constructed an overpass when I left.
I gave him flowers and he built an airport.
For traffic lights he handed out red and green
lollipops. Yet in my heart I am go children slow.

Song for a Lady

On the day of breasts and small hips
the window pocked with bad rain,
rain coming on like a minister,
we coupled, so sane and insane.
We lay like spoons while the sinister
rain dropped like flies on our lips
and our glad eyes and our small hips.

'The room is so cold with rain,' you said
and you, feminine you, with your flower
said novenas to my ankles and elbows.
You are a national product and power.
Oh my swan, my drudge, my dear wooly rose,
even a notary would notarize our bed
as you knead me and I rise like bread.

That Day

This is the desk I sit at
and this is the desk where I love you too much
and this is the typewriter that sits before me
where yesterday only your body sat before me
with its shoulders gathered in like a Greek chorus,
with its tongue like a king making up rules as he goes,
with its tongue quite openly like a cat lapping milk,
with its tongue – both of us coiled in its slippery life.
That was yesterday, that day.

That was the day of your tongue,
your tongue that came from your lips,
two openers, half animals, half birds
caught in the doorway of your heart.
That was the day I followed the king's rules,
passing by your red veins and your blue veins,
my hands down the backbone, down quick like a firepole,
hands between legs where you display your inner knowledge,
where diamond mines are buried and come forth to bury,
come forth more sudden than some reconstructed city.
It is complete within seconds, that monument.
The blood runs underground yet brings forth a tower.
A multitude should gather for such an edifice.
For a miracle one stands in line and throws confetti.
Surely The Press is here looking for headlines.
Surely someone should carry a banner on the sidewalk.
If a bridge is constructed doesn't the mayor cut a ribbon?
If a phenomenon arrives shouldn't the Magi come bearing gifts?
Yesterday was the day I bore gifts for your gift

and came from the valley to meet you on the pavement.
That was yesterday, that day.

That was the day of your face,
your face after love, close to the pillow, a lullaby.
Half asleep beside me letting the old fashioned rocker stop,
our breath became one, became a child-breath together,
while my fingers drew little o's on your shut eyes,
while my fingers drew little smiles on your mouth,
while I drew I LOVE YOU on your chest and its drummer
and whispered, 'Wake up!' and you mumbled in your sleep,
'Sh. We're driving to Cape Cod. We're heading for the Bourne
Bridge. We're circling around the Bourne Circle.' Bourne!
Then I knew you in your dream and prayed of our time
that I would be pierced and you would take root in me
and that I might bring forth your born, might bear
the you or the ghost of you in my little household.
Yesterday I did not want to be borrowed
but this is the typewriter that sits before me
and love is where yesterday is at.

Knee Song

Being kissed on the back
of the knee is a moth
at the windowscreen and
yes my darling a dot
on the fathometer is
tinkerbelle with her cough
and twice I will give up my
honor and stars will stick
like tacks in the night
yes oh yes yes two
little snails at the back
of the knee building bon-
fires something like eye-
lashes something two zippos
striking yes yes yes small
and me maker.

from Eighteen Days Without You

December 1st

As we kissed good-bye
you made a little frown.
Now Christ's lights are
twinkling all over town.
The cornstalks are broken
in the field, broken and brown.
The pond at the year's end
turns her gray eyelid down.
Christ's lights are
twinkling all over town.

A cat-green ice spreads
out over the front lawn.
The hemlocks are the only
young thing left. You are gone.
I hibernated under the covers
last night, not sleeping until dawn
came up like twilight and the oak leaves
whispered like money, those hangers on.
The hemlocks are the only
young thing left. You are gone.

December 11th

Then I think of you in bed,
your tongue half chocolate, half ocean,
of the houses that you swing into,
of the steel wool hair on your head,
of your persistent hands and then
how we gnaw at the barrier because we are two.

How you come and take my blood cup
and link me together and take my brine.
We are bare. We are stripped to the bone
and we swim in tandem and go up and up
the river, the identical river called Mine
and we enter together. No one's alone.

December 18th

Swift boomerang, come get!
I am delicate. You've been gone.
The losing has hurt me some, yet
I must bend for you. See me arch. I'm turned on.
My eyes are lawn-colored, my hair brunette.

Kiss the package, Mr. Bind!
Yes? Would you consider hurling yourself
upon me, rigorous but somehow kind?
I am laid out like paper on your cabin kitchen shelf.
So draw me a breast. I like to be underlined.

Look, lout! Say yes!
Draw me like a child. I shall need
merely two round eyes and a small kiss.
A small o. Two earrings would be nice. Then proceed
to the shoulder. You may pause at this.

Catch me. I'm your disease.
Please go slow all along the torso
drawing beads and mouths and trees
and o's, a little *graffiti* and a small *hello*
for I grab, I nibble, I lift, I please.

Draw me good, draw me warm.
Bring me your raw-boned wrist and your
strange, Mr. Bind, strange stubborn horn.
Darling, bring with this an hour of undulations, for
this is the music for which I was born.

Lock in! Be alert, my acrobat
and I will be soft wood and you the nail
and we will make fiery ovens for Jack Sprat
and you will hurl yourself into my tiny jail
and we will take a supper together and that
will be that.

from *Transformations*

(1971)

The Gold Key

The speaker in this case
is a middle-aged witch, me –
tangled on my two great arms,
my face in a book
and my mouth wide,
ready to tell you a story or two.
I have come to remind you,
all of you:
Alice, Samuel, Kurt, Eleanor,
Jane, Brian, Maryel,
all of you draw near.
Alice,
at fifty-six do you remember?
Do you remember when you
were read to as a child?
Samuel,
at twenty-two have you forgotten?
Forgotten the ten P.M. dreams
where the wicked king
went up in smoke?
Are you comatose?
Are you undersea?

Attention,
my dears,
let me present to you this boy.
He is sixteen and he wants some answers.
He is each of us.
I mean you.
I mean me.

It is not enough to read Hesse
and drink clam chowder,
we must have the answers.
The boys has found a gold key
and he is looking for what it will open.
This boy!
Upon finding a nickel
he would look for a wallet.
This boy!
Upon finding a string
he would look for a harp.
Therefore he holds the key tightly.
Its secrets whimper
like a dog in heat.
He turns the key.
Presto!
It opens this book of odd tales
which transform the Brothers Grimm.
Transform?
As if an enlarged paper clip
could be a piece of sculpture.
(And it could.)

Snow White and the Seven Dwarfs

No matter what life you lead
the virgin is a lovely number:
cheeks as fragile as cigarette paper,
arms and legs made of Limoges,
lips like Vin Du Phône,
rolling her china-blue doll eyes
open and shut.
Open to say,
Good Day Mama,
and shut for the thrust
of the unicorn.
She is unsoiled.
She is as white as a bonefish.

Once there was a lovely virgin
called Snow White.
Say she was thirteen.
Her stepmother,
a beauty in her own right,
though eaten, of course, by age,
would hear of no beauty surpassing her own.
Beauty is a simple passion,
but, oh my friends, in the end
you will dance the fire dance in iron shoes.
The stepmother had a mirror to which she referred –
something like the weather forecast –
a mirror that proclaimed
the one beauty of the land.
She would ask,
Looking glass upon the wall,

who is fairest of us all?
And the mirror would reply,
You are fairest of us all.
Pride pumped in her like poison.

Suddenly one day the mirror replied,
Queen, you are full fair, 'tis true,
but Snow White is fairer than you.
Until that moment Snow White
had been no more important
than a dust mouse under the bed.
But now the queen saw brown spots on her hand
and four whiskers over her lip
so she condemned Snow White
to be hacked to death.
Bring me her heart, she said to the hunter,
and I will salt it and eat it.
The hunter, however, let his prisoner go
and brought a boar's heart back to the castle.
The queen chewed it up like a cube steak.
Now I am fairest, she said,
lapping her slim white fingers.

Snow White walked in the wildwood
for weeks and weeks.
At each turn there were twenty doorways
and at each stood a hungry wolf,
his tongue lolling out like a worm.
The birds called out lewdly,
talking like pink parrots,
and the snakes hung down in loops,
each a noose for her sweet white neck.
On the seventh week
she came to the seventh mountain
and there she found the dwarf house.
It was as droll as a honeymoon cottage

and completely equipped with
seven beds, seven chairs, seven forks
and seven chamber pots.
Snow White ate seven chicken livers
and lay down, at last, to sleep.

The dwarfs, those little hot dogs,
walked three times around Snow White,
the sleeping virgin. They were wise
and wattled like small czars.
Yes. It's a good omen,
they said, and will bring us luck.
They stood on tiptoes to watch
Snow White wake up. She told them
about the mirror and the killer-queen
and they asked her to stay and keep house.
Beware of your stepmother,
they said.
Soon she will know you are here.
While we are away in the mines
during the day, you must not
open the door.

Looking glass upon the wall . . .
The mirror told
and so the queen dressed herself in rags
and went out like a peddler to trap Snow White.
She went across seven mountains.
She came to the dwarf house
and Snow White opened the door
and bought a bit of lacing.
The queen fastened it tightly
around her bodice,
as tight as an Ace bandage,
so tight that Snow White swooned.
She lay on the floor, a plucked daisy.

When the dwarfs came home they undid the lace
and she revived miraculously.
She was as full of life as soda pop.
Beware of your stepmother,
they said.
She will try once more.

Looking glass upon the wall . . .
Once more the mirror told
and once more the queen dressed in rags
and once more Snow White opened the door.
This time she bought a poison comb,
a curved eight-inch scorpion,
and put it in her hair and swooned again.
The dwarfs returned and took out the comb
and she revived miraculously.
She opened her eyes as wide as Orphan Annie.
Beware, beware, they said,
but the mirror told,
the queen came,
Snow White, the dumb bunny,
opened the door
and she bit into a poison apple
and fell down for the final time.
When the dwarfs returned
they undid her bodice,
they looked for a comb,
but it did no good.
Though they washed her with wine
and rubbed her with butter
it was to no avail.
She lay as still as a gold piece.

The seven dwarfs could not bring themselves
to bury her in the black ground
so they made a glass coffin

and set it upon the seventh mountain
so that all who passed by
could peek in upon her beauty.
A prince came one June day
and would not budge.
He stayed so long his hair turned green
and still he would not leave.
The dwarfs took pity upon him
and gave him the glass Snow White –
its doll's eyes shut forever –
to keep in his far-off castle.
As the prince's men carried the coffin
they stumbled and dropped it
and the chunk of apple flew out
of her throat and she woke up miraculously.

And thus Snow White became the prince's bride.
The wicked queen was invited to the wedding feast
and when she arrived there were
red-hot iron shoes,
in the manner of red-hot roller skates,
clamped upon her feet.
First your toes will smoke
and then your heels will turn black
and you will fry upward like a frog,
she was told.
And so she danced until she was dead,
a subterranean figure,
her tongue flicking in and out
like a gas jet.
Meanwhile Snow White held court,
rolling her china-blue doll eyes open and shut
and sometimes referring to her mirror
as women do.

Rapunzel

A woman
who loves a woman
is forever young.
The mentor
and the student
feed off each other.
Many a girl
had an old aunt
who locked her in the study
to keep the boys away.
They would play rummy
or lie on the couch
and touch and touch.
Old breast against young breast . . .

Let your dress fall down your shoulder,
come touch a copy of you
for I am at the mercy of rain,
for I have left the three Christs of Ypsilanti,
for I have left the long naps of Ann Arbor
and the church spires have turned to stumps.
The sea bangs into my cloister
for the young politicians are dying,
are dying so hold me, my young dear,
hold me . . .

The yellow rose will turn to cinder
and New York City will fall in
before we are done so hold me,

my young dear, hold me.
Put your pale arms around my neck.
Let me hold your heart like a flower
lest it bloom and collapse.
Give me your skin
as sheer as a cobweb,
let me open it up
and listen in and scoop out the dark.
Give me your nether lips
all puffy with their art
and I will give you angel fire in return.
We are two clouds
glistening in the bottle glass.
We are two birds
washing in the same mirror.
We were fair game
but we have kept out of the cesspool.
We are strong.
We are the good ones.
Do not discover us
for we lie together all in green
like pond weeds.
Hold me, my young dear, hold me.

They touch their delicate watches
one at a time.
They dance to the lute
two at a time.
They are as tender as bog moss.
They play mother-me-do
all day.
A woman
who loves a woman
is forever young.

Once there was a witch's garden
more beautiful than Eve's
with carrots growing like little fish,
with many tomatoes rich as frogs,
onions as ingrown as hearts,
the squash singing like a dolphin
and one patch given over wholly to magic –
rampion, a kind of salad root,
a kind of harebell more potent than penicillin,
growing leaf by leaf, skin by skin,
as rapt and as fluid as Isadora Duncan.
However the witch's garden was kept locked
and each day a woman who was with child
looked upon the rampion wildly,
fancying that she would die
if she could not have it.
Her husband feared for her welfare
and thus climbed into the garden
to fetch the life-giving tubers.

Ah ha, cried the witch,
whose proper name was Mother Gothel,
you are a thief and now you will die.
However they made a trade,
typical enough in those times.
He promised his child to Mother Gothel,
so of course when it was born
she took the child away with her.
She gave the child the name Rapunzel,
another name for the life-giving rampion.
Because Rapunzel was a beautiful girl
Mother Gothel treasured her beyond all things.
As she grew older Mother Gothel thought:
None but I will ever see her or touch her.
She locked her in a tower without a door

or a staircase. It had only a high window.
When the witch wanted to enter she cried:
Rapunzel, Rapunzel, let down your hair.
Rapunzel's hair fell to the ground like a rainbow.
It was as yellow as a dandelion
and as strong as a dog leash.
Hand over hand she shinnied up
the hair like a sailor
and there in the stone-cold room,
as cold as a museum,
Mother Gothel cried:
Hold me, my young dear, hold me,
and thus they played mother-me-do.

Years later a prince came by
and heard Rapunzel singing in her loneliness.
That song pierced his heart like a valentine
but he could find no way to get to her.
Like a chameleon he hid himself among the trees
and watched the witch ascend the swinging hair.
The next day he himself called out:
Rapunzel, Rapunzel, let down your hair,
and thus they met and he declared his love.
What is this beast, she thought,
with muscles on his arms
like a bag of snakes?
What is this moss on his legs?
What prickly plant grows on his cheeks?
What is this voice as deep as a dog?
Yet he dazzled her with his answers.
Yet he dazzled her with his dancing stick.
They lay together upon the yellowy threads,
swimming through them
like minnows through kelp
and they sang out benedictions like the Pope.

Each day he brought her a skein of silk
to fashion a ladder so they could both escape.
But Mother Gothel discovered the plot
and cut off Rapunzel's hair to her ears
and took her into the forest to repent.
When the prince came the witch fastened
the hair to a hook and let it down.
When he saw that Rapunzel had been banished
he flung himself out of the tower, a side of beef.
He was blinded by thorns that pricked him like tacks.
As blind as Oedipus he wandered for years
until he heard a song that pierced his heart
like that long-ago valentine.
As he kissed Rapunzel her tears fell on his eyes
and in the manner of such cure-alls
his sight was suddenly restored.

They lived happily as you might expect
proving that mother-me-do
can be outgrown,
just as the fish on Friday,
just as a tricycle.
The world, some say,
is made up of couples.
A rose must have a stem.

As for Mother Gothel,
her heart shrank to the size of a pin,
never again to say: Hold me, my young dear,
hold me,
and only as she dreamt of the yellow hair
did moonlight sift into her mouth.

Iron Hans

Take a lunatic
for instance,
with Saint Averton, the patron saint,
a lunatic wearing that strait jacket
like a sleeveless sweater,
singing to the wall like Muzak,
Low he walks east to west,
west to east again
like a fish in an aquarium.
And if they stripped him bare
he would fasten his hands around your throat.
After that he would take your corpse
and deposit his sperm in three orifices.
You know, I know,
you'd run away.

I am mother of the insane.
Let me give you my children:

Take a girl sitting in a chair
like a china doll.
She doesn't say a word.
She doesn't even twitch.
She's as still as furniture.
And you'll move off.

Take a man who is crying
over and over,
his face like a sponge.
You'll move off.

Take a woman talking,
purging herself with rhymes,
drumming words out like a typewriter,
planting words in you like grass seed.
You'll move off.

Take a man full of suspicions
saying: Don't touch this,
you'll be electrocuted.
Wipe off this glass three times.
There is arsenic in it.
I hear messages from God
through the fillings in my teeth.

Take a boy on a bridge.
One hundred feet up. About to jump,
thinking: This is my last ball game.
This time it's a home run.
Wanting the good crack of the bat.
Wanting to throw his body away
like a corn cob.
And you'll move off.

Take an old lady in a cafeteria
staring at the meat loaf,
crying: Mama! Mama!
And you'll move off.

Take a man in a cage
wetting his pants,
beating on that crib,
breaking his iron hands in two.
And you'll move off.

Clifford, Vincent, Friedrich,
my scooter boys,

deep in books,
long before you were mad.
Zelda, Hannah, Renée.
Moon girls,
where did you go?

There once was a king
whose forest was bewitched.
All the huntsmen,
all the hounds,
disappeared in it like soap bubbles.
A brave huntsman and his dog
entered one day to test it.
The dog drank from a black brook;
as he lapped an arm reached out
and pulled him under.
The huntsman emptied the pool
pail by pail by pail
and at the bottom lay
a wild man,
his body rusty brown.
His hair covering his knees.
Perhaps he was no more dangerous
than a hummingbird;
perhaps he was Christ's boy-child;
perhaps he was only bruised like an apple
but he appeared to them to be a lunatic.
The king placed him in a large iron cage
in the courtyard of his palace.
The court gathered around the wild man
and munched peanuts and sold balloons
and not until he cried out:
Agony! Agony!
did they move off.

The king's son
was playing with his ball one day
and it rolled into the iron cage.
It appeared as suddenly as a gallstone.
The wild man did not complain.
He talked calmly to the boy
and convinced him to unlock the cage.
The wild man carried him and his ball
piggyback off into the woods
promising him good luck and gold for life.

The wild man set the boy at a golden spring
and asked him to guard it from a fox
or a feather that might pollute it.
The boy agreed and took up residence there.
The first night he dipped his finger in.
It turned to gold; as gold as a fountain pen,
but the wild man forgave him.
The second night he bent to take a drink
and his hair got wet, turning as gold
as Midas' daughter.
As stiff as the Medusa hair of a Greek statue.
This time the wild man could not forgive him.
He sent the boy out into the world.
But if you have great need, he said,
you may come into the forest and call *Iron Hans*
and I will come to help you for you
were the only one who was kind
to this accursed bull of a wild man.

The boy went out into the world,
his gold hair tucked under a cap.
He found work as a gardener's boy
at a far-off castle. All day set out
under the red ball to dig and weed.
One day he picked some wildflowers

for the princess and took them to her.
She demanded he take off his cap
in her presence. You look like a jester,
she taunted him, but he would not.
You look like a bird, she taunted him,
and snatched off the cap.
His hair fell down with a clang.
It fell down like a moon chain
and it delighted her.
The princess fell in love.

Next there was a war
that the king was due to lose.
The boy went into the forest
and called out: Iron Hans, Iron Hans,
and the wild man appeared.
He gave the boy a black charger,
a sword as sharp as a guillotine
and a great body of black knights.
They went forth and cut the enemy down
like a row of cabbage heads.
Then they vanished.
The court talked of nothing
but the unknown knight in a cap.
The princess thought of the boy
but the head gardener said:
Not he. He had only a three-legged horse.
He could have done better with a stork.
Three days in a row,
the princess, hoping to lure him back,
threw a gold ball.
Remember back,
the boy was good at losing balls
but was he good at catching them?
Three days running the boy,
thanks to Iron Hans,

performed like Joe Dimaggio.
And thus they were married.

At the wedding feast
the music stopped suddenly
and a door flew open
and a proud king walked in
and embraced the boy.
Of course
it was Iron Hans.
He had been bewitched
and the boy had broken the spell.
He who slays the warrior
and captures the maiden's heart
undoes the spell.
He who kills his father
and thrice wins his mother
undoes the spell.

Without Thorazine
or benefit of psychotherapy
Iron Hans was transformed.
No need for Master Medical;
no need for electroshock –
merely bewitched all along.
Just as the frog who was a prince.
Just as the madman his simple boyhood.

When I was a wild man,
Iron Hans said,
I tarnished all the world.
I was the infector.
I was the poison breather.
I was a professional,
but you have saved me
from the awful babble
of that calling.

The Little Peasant

Oh how the women
grip and stretch
fainting on the horn.

The men and women
cry to each other.
Touch me,
my pancake,
and make me young.
And thus
like many of us,
the parson
and the miller's wife
lie down in sin.

The women cry,
Come, my fox,
heal me.
I am chalk white
with middle age
so wear me threadbare,
wear me down,
wear me out.
Lick me clean,
as clean as an almond.

The men cry,
Come, my lily,
my fringy queen,
my gaudy dear,

salt me a bird
and be its noose.
Bounce me off
like a shuttlecock.
Dance me dingo-sweet
for I am your lizard,
your sly thing.

Long ago
there was a peasant
who was poor but crafty.
He was not yet a voyeur.
He had yet to find
the miller's wife
at her game.
Now he had not enough
cabbage for supper
nor clover for his one cow.
So he slaughtered the cow
and took the skin
to town.
It was worth no more
than a dead fly
but he hoped for profit.

On his way
he came upon a raven
with damaged wings.
It lay as crumpled as
a wet washcloth.
He said, Come little fellow,
you're part of my booty.

On his way
there was a fierce storm.
Hail jabbed the little peasant's cheeks

like toothpicks.
So he sought shelter at the miller's house.
The miller's wife gave him only
a hunk of stale bread
and let him lie down on some straw.
The peasant wrapped himself and the raven
up in the cowhide
and pretended to fall asleep.

When he lay
as still as a sausage
the miller's wife
let in the parson, saying,
My husband is out
so we shall have a feast.
Roast meat, salad, cakes and wine.
The parson,
his eyes as black as caviar,
said, Come, my lily,
my fringy queen.
The miller's wife,
her lips as red as pimientos,
said, Touch me, my pancake,
and wake me up.
And thus they ate.
And thus
they dingoed-sweet.

Then the miller
was heard stomping on the doorstep
and the miller's wife
hid the food about the house
and the parson in the cupboard.

The miller asked, upon entering,
What is that dead cow doing in the corner?

The peasant spoke up.
It is mine.
I sought shelter from the storm.
You are welcome, said the miller,
but my stomach is as empty as a flour sack.
His wife told him she had no food
but bread and cheese.
So be it, the miller said,
and the three of them ate.

The miller looked once more
at the cowskin
and asked its purpose.
The peasant answered,
I hide my soothsayer in it.
He knows five things about you
but the fifth he keeps to himself.
The peasant pinched the raven's head
and it croaked, Krr. Krr.
That means, translated the peasant,
there is wine under the pillow.
And there it sat
as warm as a specimen.

Krr. Krr.
They found the roast meat under the stove.
It lay there like an old dog.
Krr. Krr.
They found the salad in the bed
and the cakes under it.
Krr. Krr.

Because of all this
the miller burned to know the fifth thing.
How much? he asked,
little caring he was being milked.

They settled on a large sum
and the soothsayer said,
The devil is in the cupboard.
And the miller unlocked it.
Krr. Krr.

There stood the parson,
rigid for a moment,
as real as a soup can
and then he took off like a fire
with the wind at its back.
I have tricked the devil,
cried the miller with delight,
and I have tweaked his chin whiskers.
I will be as famous as the king.

The miller's wife
smiled to herself.
Though never again to dingo-sweet
her secret was as safe
as a fly in an outhouse.

The sly little peasant
strode home the next morning,
a soothsayer over his shoulder
and gold pieces knocking like marbles
in his deep pants pocket.
Krr. Krr.

Briar Rose (Sleeping Beauty)

Consider
a girl who keeps slipping off,
arms limp as old carrots,
into the hypnotist's trance,
into a spirit world
speaking with the gift of tongues.
She is stuck in the time machine,
suddenly two years old sucking her thumb,
as inward as a snail,
learning to talk again.
She's on a voyage.
She is swimming further and further back,
up like a salmon,
struggling into her mother's pocketbook.
Little doll child,
come here to Papa.
Sit on my knee.
I have kisses for the back of your neck.
A penny for your thoughts, Princess.
I will hunt them like an emerald.
Come be my snooky
and I will give you a root.
That kind of voyage,
rank as honeysuckle.

Once
a king had a christening
for his daughter Briar Rose
and because he had only twelve gold plates
he asked only twelve fairies

to the grand event.
The thirteenth fairy,
her fingers as long and thin as straws,
her eyes burnt by cigarettes,
her uterus an empty teacup,
arrived with an evil gift.
She made this prophecy:
The princess shall prick herself
on a spinning wheel in her fifteenth year
and then fall down dead.
Kaputt!
The court fell silent.
The king looked like Munch's *Scream*.
Fairies' prophecies,
in times like those,
held water.
However the twelfth fairy
had a certain kind of eraser
and thus she mitigated the curse
changing that death
into a hundred-year sleep.

The king ordered every spinning wheel
exterminated and exorcized.
Briar Rose grew to be a goddess
and each night the king
bit the hem of her gown
to keep her safe.
He fastened the moon up
with a safety pin
to give her perpetual light.
He forced every male in the court
to scour his tongue with Bab-o
lest they poison the air she dwelt in.
Thus she dwelt in his odor.
Rank as honeysuckle.

On her fifteenth birthday
she pricked her finger
on a charred spinning wheel
and the clocks stopped.
Yes indeed. She went to sleep.
The king and queen went to sleep,
the courtiers, the flies on the wall.
The fire in the hearth grew still
and the roast meat stopped crackling.
The trees turned into metal
and the dog became china.
They all lay in a trance,
each a catatonic
stuck in the time machine.
Even the frogs were zombies.
Only a bunch of briar roses grew
forming a great wall of tacks
around the castle.
Many princes
tried to get through the brambles
for they had heard much of Briar Rose
but they had not scoured their tongues
so they were held by the thorns
and thus were crucified.
In due time
a hundred years passed
and a prince got through.
The briars parted as if for Moses
and the prince found the tableau intact.
He kissed Briar Rose
and she woke up crying:
Daddy! Daddy!
Presto! She's out of prison!
She married the prince
and all went well

except for the fear –
the fear of sleep.

Briar Rose
was an insomniac . . .
She could not nap
or lie in sleep
without the court chemist
mixing her some knock-out drops
and never in the prince's presence.
If it is to come, she said,
sleep must take me unawares
while I am laughing or dancing
so that I do not know that brutal place
where I lie down with cattle prods
the hole in my cheek open.
Further, I must not dream
for when I do I see the table set
and a faltering crone at my place,
her eyes burnt by cigarettes
as she eats betrayal like a slice of meat.

I must not sleep
for while asleep I'm ninety
and think I'm dying.
Death rattles in my throat
like a marble.
I wear tubes like earrings.
I lie as still as a bar of iron.
You can stick a needle
through my kneecap and I won't flinch.
I'm all shot up with Novocain.
This trance girl
is yours to do with.
You could lay her in a grave,

an awful package,
and shovel dirt on her face
and she'd never call back: Hello there!
But if you kissed her on the mouth
her eyes would spring open
and she'd call out: Daddy! Daddy!
Presto!
She's out of prison.

There was a theft.
That much I am told.
I was abandoned.
That much I know.
I was forced backward.
I was forced forward.
I was passed hand to hand
like a bowl of fruit.
Each night I am nailed into place
and I forget who I am.
Daddy?
That's another kind of prison.
It's not the prince at all,
but my father
drunkenly bent over my bed,
circling the abyss like a shark,
my father thick upon me
like some sleeping jellyfish.
What voyage this, little girl?
This coming out of prison?
God help –
this life after death?

from *The Book of Folly*

(1972)

The Ambition Bird

So it has come to this –
insomnia at 3:15 A.M.,
the clock tolling its engine

like a frog following
a sundial yet having an electric
seizure at the quarter hour.

The business of words keeps me awake.
I am drinking cocoa,
that warm brown mama.

I would like a simple life
yet all night I am laying
poems away in a long box.

It is my immortality box,
my lay-away plan,
my coffin.

All night dark wings
flopping in my heart.
Each an ambition bird.

The bird wants to be dropped
from a high place like Tallahatchie Bridge.

He wants to light a kitchen match
and immolate himself.

He wants to fly into the hand of Michelangelo
and come out painted on a ceiling.

He wants to pierce the hornet's nest
and come out with a long godhead.

He wants to take bread and wine
and bring forth a man happily floating in the Caribbean.

He wants to be pressed out like a key
so he can unlock the Magi.

He wants to take leave among strangers
passing out bits of his heart like hors d'oeuvres.

He wants to die changing his clothes
and bolt for the sun like a diamond.

He wants, I want.
Dear God, wouldn't it be
good enough to just drink cocoa?

I must get a new bird
and a new immortality box.
There is folly enough inside this one.

Mother and Daughter

Linda, you are leaving
your old body now.
It lies flat, an old butterfly,
all arm, all leg, all wing,
loose as an old dress.
I reach out toward it but
my fingers turn to cankers
and I am motherwarm and used,
just as your childhood is used.
Question you about this
and you hold up pearls.
Question you about this
and you pass by armies.
Question you about this –
you with your big clock going,
its hands wider than jackstraws –
and you'll sew up a continent.

Now that you are eighteen
I give you my booty, my spoils,
my Mother & Co. and my ailments.
Question you about this
and you'll not know the answer –
the muzzle at the mouth,
the hopeful tent of oxygen,
the tubes, the pathways,
the war and the war's vomit.
Keep on, keep on, keep on,
carrying keepsakes to the boys,

carrying powders to the boys,
carrying, my Linda, blood to
the bloodletter.

Linda, you are leaving
your old body now.
You've picked my pocket clean
and you've racked up all my
poker chips and left me empty
and, as the river between us
narrows, you do calisthenics,
that womanly leggy semaphore.
Question you about this
and you will sew me a shroud
and hold up Monday's broiler
and thumb out the chicken gut.
Question you about this
and you will see my death
drooling at these gray lips
while you, my burglar, will eat
fruit and pass the time of day.

The Wifebeater

There will be mud on the carpet tonight
and blood in the gravy as well.
The wifebeater is out,
the childbeater is out
eating soil and drinking bullets from a cup.
He strides back and forth
in front of my study window
chewing little red pieces of my heart.
His eyes flash like a birthday cake
and he makes bread out of rock.

Yesterday he was walking
like a man in the world.
He was upright and conservative
but somehow evasive, somehow contagious.
Yesterday he built me a country
and laid out a shadow where I could sleep
but today a coffin for the madonna and child,
today two women in baby clothes will be hamburg.

With a tongue like a razor he will kiss,
the mother, the child,
and we three will color the stars black
in memory of his mother
who kept him chained to the food tree
or turned him on and off like a water faucet
and made *women* through all these hazy years
the enemy with a heart of lies.

Tonight all the red dogs lie down in fear
and the wife and daughter knit into each other
until they are killed.

from The Death of the Fathers

1. Oysters

Oysters we ate,
sweet blue babies,
twelve eyes looked up at me,
running with lemon and Tabasco.
I was afraid to eat this father-food
and Father laughed
and drank down his martini,
clear as tears.
It was a soft medicine
that came from the sea into my mouth,
moist and plump.
I swallowed.
It went down like a large pudding.
Then I ate one o'clock and two o'clock.
Then I laughed and then we laughed
and let me take note –
there was a death,
the death of childhood
there at the Union Oyster House
for I was fifteen
and eating oysters
and the child was defeated.
The woman won.

2. How We Danced

The night of my cousin's wedding
I wore blue.
I was nineteen
and we danced, Father, we orbited.
We moved like angels washing themselves.
We moved like two birds on fire.
Then we moved like the sea in a jar,
slower and slower.
The orchestra played
'Oh how we danced on the night we were wed.'
And you waltzed me like a lazy Susan
and we were dear,
very dear.
Now that you are laid out,
useless as a blind dog,
now that you no longer lurk,
the song rings in my head.
Pure oxygen was the champagne we drank
and clicked our glasses, one to one.
The champagne breathed like a skin diver
and the glasses were crystal and the bride
and groom gripped each other in sleep
like nineteen-thirty marathon dancers.
Mother was a belle and danced with twenty men.
You danced with me never saying a word.
Instead the serpent spoke as you held me close.
The serpent, that mocker, woke up and pressed against me
like a great god and we bent together
like two lonely swans.

4. Santa

Father,
the Santa Claus suit
you bought from Wolf Fording Theatrical Supplies,
back before I was born,
is dead.
The white beard you fooled me with
and the hair like Moses,
the thick crimpy wool
that used to buzz me on the neck,
is dead.
Yes, my busting rosy Santa,
ringing your bronze cowbell.
You with real soot on your nose
and snow (taken from the refrigerator some years)
on your big shoulder.
The room was like Florida.
You took so many oranges out of your bag
and threw them around the living room,
all the time laughing that North Pole laugh.
Mother would kiss you
for she was that tall.
Mother could hug you
for she was not afraid.
The reindeer pounded on the roof.
(It was my Nana with a hammer in the attic.
For my children it was my husband
with a crowbar breaking things up.)
The year I ceased to believe in you
is the year you were drunk.
My boozy red man,
your voice all slithery like soap,

you were a long way from Saint Nick
with Daddy's cocktail smell.
I cried and ran from the room
and you said, 'Well, thank God that's over!'
And it was, until the grandchildren came.
Then I tied up your pillows
in the five A.M. Christ morning
and I adjusted the beard,
all yellow with age,
and applied rouge to your cheeks
and Chalk White to your eyebrows.
We were conspirators,
secret actors,
and I kissed you
because I was tall enough.
But that is over.
The era closes
and large children hang their stockings
and build a black memorial to you.
And you, you fade out of sight
like a lost signalman
wagging his lantern
for the train that comes no more.

from The Jesus Papers

Jesus Raises Up the Harlot

The harlot squatted
with her hands over her red hair.
She was not looking for customers.
She was in a deep fear.
A delicate body clothed in red,
as red as a smashed fist
and she was bloody as well
for the townspeople were trying
to stone her to death.
Stones came at her like bees to candy
and sweet redheaded harlot that she was
she screamed out, *I never, I never.*
Rocks flew out of her mouth like pigeons
and Jesus saw this and thought to
exhume her like a mortician.

Jesus knew that a terrible sickness
dwelt in the harlot and He could lance it
with His two small thumbs.
He held up His hand and the stones
dropped to the ground like doughnuts.
Again He held up His hand
and the harlot came and kissed Him.
He lanced her twice. On the spot.
He lanced her twice on each breast,
pushing His thumbs in until the milk ran out,

those two boils of whoredom.
The harlot followed Jesus around like a puppy
for He had raised her up.
Now she forsook her fornications
and became His pet.
His raising her up made her feel
like a little girl again when she had a father
who brushed the dirt from her eye.
Indeed, she took hold of herself,
knowing she owed Jesus a life,
as sure-fire as a trump card.

Jesus Cooks

Jesus saw the multitudes were hungry
and He said, Oh Lord,
send down a short-order cook.
And the Lord said, Abracadabra.
Jesus took the fish,
a slim green baby,
in His right hand and said, Oh Lord,
and the Lord said,
Work on the sly
opening boxes of sardine cans.
And He did.
Fisherman, fisherman,
you make it look easy.
And lo, there were many fish.
Next Jesus held up a loaf
and said, Oh Lord,
and the Lord instructed Him
like an assembly-line baker man,
a Pied Piper of yeast,
and lo, there were many.

Jesus passed among the people
in a chef's hat
and they kissed His spoons and forks
and ate well from invisible dishes.

Jesus Dies

From up here in the crow's nest
I see a small crowd gather.
Why do you gather, my townsmen?
There is no news here.
I am not a trapeze artist.
I am busy with My dying.
Three heads lolling,
bobbing like bladders.
No news.
The soldiers down below
laughing as soldiers have done for centuries.
No news.
We are the same men,
you and I,
the same sort of nostrils,
the same sort of feet.
My bones are oiled with blood
and so are yours.
My heart pumps like a jack rabbit in a trap
and so does yours.
I want to kiss God on His nose and watch Him sneeze
and so do you.
Not out of disrespect.
Out of pique.
Out of a man-to-man thing.
I want heaven to descend and sit on My dinner plate
and so do you.
I want God to put His steaming arms around Me

and so do you.
Because we need.
Because we are sore creatures.
My townsmen,
go home now.
I will do nothing extraordinary.
I will not divide in two.
I will not pick out My white eyes.
Go now,
this is a personal matter,
a private affair and God knows
none of your business.

from *The Death Notebooks*

(1974)

For Mr. Death who Stands with His Door Open

Time grows dim. Time that was so long
grows short, time, all goggle-eyed,
wiggling her skirts, singing her torch song,
giving the boys a buzz and a ride,
that Nazi Mama with her beer and sauerkraut.
Time, old gal of mine, will soon dim out.

May I say how young she was back then,
playing piggley-witch and hoola-hoop,
dancing the jango with six awful men,
letting the chickens out of the coop,
promising to marry Jack and Jerome,
and never bothering, never, never,
to come back home.

Time was when time had time enough
and the sea washed me daily in its delicate brine.
There is no terror when you swim in the buff
or speed up the boat and hang out a line.
Time was when I could hiccup and hold my breath
and not in that instant meet Mr. Death.

Mr. Death, you actor, you have many masks.
Once you were sleek, a kind of Valentino
with my father's bathtub gin in your flask.
With my cinched-in waist and my dumb vertigo
at the crook of your long white arm
and yet you never bent me back, never, never,
into your blackguard charm.

Next, Mr. Death, you held out the bait
during my first decline, as they say,
telling that suicide baby to celebrate
her own going in her own puppet play.
I went out popping pills and crying adieu
in my own death camp with my own little Jew.

Now your beer belly hangs out like Fatso.
You are popping your buttons and expelling gas.
How can I lie down with you, my comical beau
when you are so middle-aged and lower-class.
Yet you'll press me down in your envelope;
pressed as neat as a butterfly, forever, forever,
beside Mussolini and the Pope.

Mr. Death, when you came to the ovens it was short
and to the drowning man you were likewise kind,
and the nicest of all to the baby I had to abort
and middling you were to all the crucified combined.
But when it comes to my death let it be slow,
let it be pantomime, this last peep show,
so that I may squat at the edge trying on
my black necessary trousseau.

from The Furies

The Fury of Guitars and Sopranos

This singing
is a kind of dying,
a kind of birth,
a votive candle.
I have a dream-mother
who sings with her guitar,
nursing the bedroom
with moonlight and beautiful olives.
A flute came too,
joining the five strings,
a God finger over the holes.
I knew a beautiful woman once
who sang with her fingertips
and her eyes were brown
like small birds.
At the cup of her breasts
I drew wine.
At the mound of her legs
I drew figs.
She sang for my thirst,
mysterious songs of God
that would have laid an army down.
It was as if a morning-glory
had bloomed in her throat
and all that blue
and small pollen
ate into my heart
violent and religious.

The Fury of Cooks

Herbs, garlic,
cheese, please let me in!
Souffles, salads,
Parker House rolls,
please let me in!
Cook Helen,
why are you so cross,
why is your kitchen verboten?
Couldn't you just teach me
to bake a potato,
that charm,
that young prince?
No! No!
This is my country!
You shout silently.
Couldn't you just show me
the gravy. How you drill it out
of the stomach of that bird?
Helen, Helen,
let me in,
let me feel the flour,
is it blind and frightening,
this stuff that makes cakes?
Helen, Helen,
the kitchen is your dog
and you pat it
and love it
and keep it clean.

But all these things,
all these dishes of things
come through the swinging door
and I don't know from where?
Give me some tomato aspic, Helen!
I don't want to be alone.

The Fury of Cocks

There they are
drooping over the breakfast plates,
angel-like,
folding in their sad wing,
animal sad,
and only the night before
there they were
playing the banjo.
Once more the day's light comes
with its immense sun,
its mother trucks,
its engines of amputation.
Whereas last night
the cock knew its way home,
as stiff as a hammer,
battering in with all
its awful power.
That theater.
Today it is tender,
a small bird,
as soft as a baby's hand.
She is the house.
He is the steeple.
When they fuck they are God.
When they break away they are God.
When they snore they are God.
In the morning they butter the toast.
They don't say much.

They are still God.
All the cocks of the world are God,
blooming, blooming, blooming
into the sweet blood of woman.

The Fury of Overshoes

They sit in a row
outside the kindergarten,
black, red, brown, all
with those brass buckles.
Remember when you couldn't
buckle your own
overshoe
or tie your own
shoe
or cut your own meat
and the tears
running down like mud
because you fell off your
tricycle?
Remember, big fish,
when you couldn't swim
and simply slipped under
like a stone frog?
The world wasn't
yours.
It belonged to
the big people.
Under your bed
sat the wolf
and he made a shadow
when cars passed by
at night.
They made you give up

your nightlight
and your teddy
and your thumb.
Oh overshoes,
don't you
remember me,
pushing you up and down
in the winter snow?
Oh thumb,
I want a drink,
it is dark,
where are the big people,
when will I get there,
taking giant steps
all day,
each day
and thinking
nothing of it?

The Fury of Sunrises

Darkness
as black as your eyelid,
poketricks of stars,
the yellow mouth,
the smell of a stranger,
dawn coming up,
dark blue,
no stars,
the smell of a lover,
warmer now
as authentic as soap,
wave after wave
of lightness
and the birds in their chains
going mad with throat noises,
the birds in their tracks
yelling into their cheeks like clowns,
lighter, lighter,
the stars gone,
the trees appearing in their green hoods,
the house appearing across the way,
the road and its sad macadam,
the rock walls losing their cotton,
lighter, lighter,
letting the dog out and seeing
fog lift by her legs,
a gauze dance,
lighter, lighter,

yellow, blue at the tops of trees,
more God, more God everywhere,
lighter, lighter,
more world everywhere,
sheets bent back for people,
the strange heads of love
and breakfast,
that sacrament,
lighter, yellower,
like the yolk of eggs,
the flies gathering at the windowpane,
the dog inside whining for food
and the day commencing,
not to die, not to die,
as in the last day breaking,
a final day digesting itself,
lighter, lighter,
the endless colors,
the same old trees stepping toward me,
the rock unpacking its crevices,
breakfast like a dream
and the whole day to live through,
steadfast, deep, interior.
After the death,
after the black of black,
this lightness –
not to die, not to die –
that God begot.

from O Ye Tongues

First Psalm

Let there be a God as large as a sunlamp to laugh his heat at you.

Let there be an earth with a form like a jigsaw and let it fit for all of ye.

Let there be the darkness of a darkroom out of the deep. A worm room.

Let there be a God who sees light at the end of a long thin pipe and lets it in.

Let God divide them in half.

Let God share his Hoodsie.

Let the waters divide so that God may wash his face in first light.

Let there be pin holes in the sky in which God puts his little finger.

Let the stars be a heaven of jelly rolls and babies laughing.

Let the light be called Day so that men may grow corn or take busses.

Let there be on the second day dry land so that all men may dry their toes with Cannon towels.

Let God call this earth and feel the grasses rise up like angel hair.

Let there be bananas, cucumbers, prunes, mangoes, beans, rice and candy canes.

Let them seed and reseed.

Let there be seasons so that we may learn the architecture of the sky with eagles, finches, flickers, seagulls.

Let there be seasons so that we may put on twelve coats and shovel snow or take off our skins and bathe in the Carribean.

Let there be seasons so that sky dogs will jump across the sun in December.

Let there be seasons so that the eel may come out of her green cave.

Let there be seasons so that the raccoon may raise his blood level.

Let there be seasons so that the wind may be hoisted for an orange leaf.

Let there be seasons so that the rain will bury many ships.

Let there be seasons so that the miracles will fill our drinking glass with runny gold.

Let there be seasons so that our tongues will be rich in asparagus and limes.

Let there be seasons so that our fires will not forsake us and turn to metal.

Let there be seasons so that a man may close his palm on a woman's breast and bring forth a sweet nipple, a starberry.

Let there be a heaven so that man may outlive his grasses.

Tenth Psalm

For as the baby springs out like a starfish into her million light years Anne sees that she must climb her own mountain.

For as she eats wisdom like the halves of a pear she puts one foot in front of the other. She climbs the dark wing.

For as her child grows Anne grows and there is salt and cantaloupe and molasses for all.

For as Anne walks, the music walks and the family lies down in milk.

For I am not locked up.

For I am placing fist over fist on rock and plunging into the altitude of words. The silence of words.

For the husband sells his rain to God and God is well pleased with His family.

For they fling together against hardness and somewhere, in another room, a light is clicked on by gentle fingers.

For death comes to friends, to parents, to sisters. Death comes with its bagful of pain yet they do not curse the key they were given to hold.

For they open each door and it gives them a new day at the yellow window.

For the child grows to a woman, her breasts coming up like the moon while Anne rubs the peace stone.

For the child starts up her own mountain (not being locked in) and reaches the coastline of grapes.

For Anne and her daughter master the mountain and again and again. Then the child finds a man who opens like the sea.

For that daughter must build her own city and fill it with her own oranges, her own words.

For Anne walked up and up and finally over the years until she was old as the moon and with its naggy voice.

For Anne had climbed over eight mountains and saw the children washing the tiny statues in the square.

For Anne sat down with the blood of a hammer and built a tombstone for herself and Christopher sat beside her and was well pleased with their red shadow.

For they hung up a picture of a rat and the rat smiled and held out his hand.

For the rat was blessed on that mountain. He was given a white bath.

For the milk in the skies sank down upon them and tucked them in.

For God did not forsake them but put the blood angel to look after them until such time as they would enter their star.

For the sky dogs jumped out and shoveled snow upon us and we lay in our quiet blood.

For God was as large as a sunlamp and laughed his heat at us and therefore we did not cringe at the death hole.

Jesus Walking

When Jesus walked into the wilderness
he carried a man on his back,
at least it had the form of a man,
a fisherman perhaps with a wet nose,
a baker perhaps with flour in his eyes.
The man was dead it seems
and yet he was unkillable.
Jesus carried many men
yet there was only one man –
if indeed it was a man.
There in the wilderness all the leaves
reached out their hands
but Jesus went on by.
The bees beckoned him to their honey
but Jesus went on by.
The boar cut out its heart and offered it
but Jesus went on by
with his heavy burden.
The devil approached and slapped him on the jaw
and Jesus walked on.
The devil made the earth move like an elevator
and Jesus walked on.
The devil built a city of whores,
each in little angel beds,
and Jesus walked on with his burden.
For forty days, for forty nights
Jesus put one foot in front of the other
and the man he carried,
if it was a man,
became heavier and heavier.

He was carrying all the trees of the world
which are one tree.
He was carrying forty moons
which are one moon.
He was carrying all the boots
of all the men in the world
which are one boot.
He was carrying our blood.
One blood.

To pray, Jesus knew,
is to be a man carrying a man.

from *The Awful Rowing Toward God*
(1975)

Rowing

A story, a story!
(Let it go. Let it come.)
I was stamped out like a Plymouth fender
into this world.
First came the crib
with its glacial bars.
Then dolls
and the devotion to their plastic mouths.
Then there was school,
the little straight rows of chairs,
blotting my name over and over,
but undersea all the time,
a stranger whose elbows wouldn't work.
Then there was life
with its cruel houses
and people who seldom touched –
though touch is all –
but I grew,
like a pig in a trenchcoat I grew,
and then there were many strange apparitions,
the nagging rain, the sun turning into poison
and all of that, saws working through my heart,
but I grew, I grew,
and God was there like an island I had not rowed to,
still ignorant of Him, my arms and my legs worked,
and I grew, I grew,
I wore rubies and bought tomatoes
and now, in my middle age,
about nineteen in the head I'd say,
I am rowing, I am rowing

though the oarlocks stick and are rusty
and the sea blinks and roils
like a worried eyeball,
but I am rowing, I am rowing,
though the wind pushes me back
and I know that that island will not be perfect,
it will have the flaws of life,
the absurdities of the dinner table,
but there will be a door
and I will open it
and I will get rid of the rat inside of me,
the gnawing pestilential rat.
God will take it with his two hands
and embrace it.

As the African says:
This is my tale which I have told,
if it be sweet, if it be not sweet,
take somewhere else and let some return to me.
This story ends with me still rowing.

The Civil War

I am torn in two
but I will conquer myself.
I will dig up the pride.
I will take scissors
and cut out the beggar.
I will take a crowbar
and pry out the broken
pieces of God in me.
Just like a jigsaw puzzle,
I will put Him together again
with the patience of a chess player.

How many pieces?

It feels like thousands,
God dressed up like a whore
in a slime of green algae.
God dressed up like an old man
staggering out of His shoes.
God dressed up like a child,
all naked,
even without skin,
soft as an avocado when you peel it.
And others, others, others.

But I will conquer them all
and build a whole nation of God
in me – but united,
build a new soul,

dress it with skin
and then put on my shirt
and sing an anthem,
a song of myself.

Courage

It is in the small things we see it.
The child's first step,
as awesome as an earthquake.
The first time you rode a bike,
wallowing up the sidewalk.
The first spanking when your heart
went on a journey all alone.
When they called you crybaby
or poor or fatty or crazy
and made you into an alien,
you drank their acid
and concealed it.

Later,
if you faced the death of bombs and bullets
you did not do it with a banner,
you did it with only a hat to
cover your heart.
You did not fondle the weakness inside you
though it was there.
Your courage was a small coal
that you kept swallowing.
If your buddy saved you
and died himself in so doing,
then his courage was not courage,
it was love; love as simple as shaving soap.

Later,
if you have endured a great despair,
then you did it alone,

getting a transfusion from the fire,
picking the scabs off your heart,
then wringing it out like a sock.
Next, my kinsman, you powdered your sorrow,
you gave it a back rub
and then you covered it with a blanket
and after it had slept a while
it woke to the wings of the roses
and was transformed.

Later,
when you face old age and its natural conclusion
your courage will still be shown in the little ways,
each spring will be a sword you'll sharpen,
those you love will live in a fever of love,
and you'll bargain with the calendar
and at the last moment
when death opens the back door
you'll put on your carpet slippers
and stride out.

When Man Enters Woman

When man
enters woman,
like the surf biting the shore,
again and again,
and the woman opens her mouth in pleasure
and her teeth gleam
like the alphabet,
Logos appears milking a star,
and the man
inside of woman
ties a knot
so that they will
never again be separate
and the woman
climbs into a flower
and swallows its stem
and Logos appears
and unleashes their rivers.

This man,
this woman
with their double hunger,
have tried to reach through
the curtain of God
and briefly they have,
though God
in His perversity
unties the knot.

The Earth

God loafs around heaven,
without a shape
but He would like to smoke His cigar
or bite His fingernails
and so forth.

God owns heaven
but He craves the earth,
the earth with its little sleepy caves,
its bird resting at the kitchen window,
even its murders lined up like broken chairs,
even its writers digging into their souls
with jackhammers.
even its hucksters selling their animals
for gold,
even its babies sniffing for their music,
the farm house, white as a bone,
sitting in the lap of its corn,
even the statue holding up its widowed life,
even the ocean with its cupful of students,
but most of all He envies the bodies,
He who has no body.

The eyes, opening and shutting like keyholes
and never forgetting, recording by thousands,
the skull with its brains like eels –
the tablet of the world –
the bones and their joints
that build and break for any trick,
the genitals,

the ballast of the eternal,
and the heart, of course,
that swallows the tides
and spits them out cleansed.

He does not envy the soul so much.
He is all soul
but He would like to house it in a body
and come down
and give it a bath
now and then.

The Dead Heart

After I wrote this, a friend scrawled on this page, 'Yes.'

And I said, merely to myself, 'I wish it could be for a different
seizure – as with Molly Bloom with her "and yes I said yes I will Yes." '

It is not a turtle
hiding in its little green shell.
It is not a stone
to pick up and put under your black wing.
It is not a subway car that is obsolete.
It is not a lump of coal that you could light.
It is a dead heart.
It is inside of me.
It is a stranger
yet once it was agreeable,
opening and closing like a clam.

What it has cost me you can't imagine,
shrinks, priests, lovers, children, husbands,
friends and all the lot.
An expensive thing it was to keep going.
It gave back too.
Don't deny it!
I half wonder if April would bring it back to life?
A tulip? The first bud?
But those are just musings on my part,
the pity one has when one looks at a cadaver.

How did it die?
I called it EVIL.
I said to it, your poems stink like vomit.
I didn't stay to hear the last sentence.

It died on the word EVIL.
I did it with my tongue.
The tongue, the Chinese say,
is like a sharp knife:
it kills
without drawing blood.

The Sickness Unto Death

God went out of me
as if the sea dried up like sandpaper,
as if the sun became a latrine.
God went out of my fingers.
They became stone.
My body became a side of mutton
and despair roamed the slaughterhouse.

Someone brought me oranges in my despair
but I could not eat a one
for God was in that orange.
I could not touch what did not belong to me.
The priest came,
he said God was even in Hitler.
I did not believe him
for if God were in Hitler
then God would be in me.
I did not hear the bird sounds.
They had left.

I did not see the speechless clouds,
I saw only the little white dish of my faith
breaking in the crater.
I kept saying:
I've got to have something to hold on to.
People gave me Bibles, crucifixes,
a yellow daisy,
but I could not touch them,
I who was a house full of bowel movement,

I who was a defaced altar,
I who wanted to crawl toward God
could not move nor eat bread.

So I ate myself,
bite by bite,
and the tears washed me,
wave after cowardly wave,
swallowing canker after canker
and Jesus stood over me looking down
and He laughed to find me gone,
and put His mouth to mine
and gave me His air.

My kindred, my brother, I said
and gave the yellow daisy
to the crazy woman in the next bed.

Welcome Morning

There is joy
in all:
in the hair I brush each morning,
in the Cannon towel, newly washed,
that I rub my body with each morning,
in the chapel of eggs I cook
each morning,
in the outcry from the kettle
that heats my coffee
each morning,
in the spoon and the chair
that cry 'hello there, Anne'
each morning,
in the godhead of the table
that I set my silver, plate, cup upon
each morning.

All this is God,
right here in my pea-green house
each morning
and I mean,
though often forget,
to give thanks,
to faint down by the kitchen table
in a prayer of rejoicing
as the holy birds at the kitchen window
peck into their marriage of seeds.

So while I think of it,
let me paint a thank-you on my palm
for this God, this laughter of the morning,
lest it go unspoken.

The Joy that isn't shared, I've heard,
dies young.

Frenzy

I am not lazy.
I am on the amphetamine of the soul.
I am, each day,
typing out the God
my typewriter believes in.
Very quick. Very intense,
like a wolf at a live heart.

Not lazy.
When a lazy man, they say,
looks toward heaven,
the angels close the windows.

Oh angels,
keep the windows open
so that I may reach in
and steal each object,
objects that tell me the sea is not dying,
objects that tell me the dirt has a life-wish,
that the Christ who walked for me,
walked on true ground
and that this frenzy,
like bees stinging the heart all morning,
will keep the angels
with their windows open,
wide as an English bathtub.

The Rowing Endeth

I'm mooring my rowboat
at the dock of the island called God.
This dock is made in the shape of a fish
and there are many boats moored
at many different docks.
'It's okay,' I say to myself,
with blisters that broke and healed
and broke and healed –
saving themselves over and over.
And salt sticking to my face and arms like
a glue-skin pocked with grains of tapioca.
I empty myself from my wooden boat
and onto the flesh of The Island.
'On with it!' He says and thus
we squat on the rocks by the sea
and play—can it be true—
a game of poker.
He calls me.
I win because I hold a royal straight flush.
He wins because He holds five aces.
A wild card had been announced
but I had not heard it
being in such a state of awe
when He took out the cards and dealt.
As he plunks down His five aces
and I sit grinning at my royal flush,
He starts to laugh,
the laughter rolling like a hoop out of His mouth
and into mine,
and such laughter that He doubles right over me

laughing a Rejoice-Chorus at our two triumphs.
Then I laugh, the fishy dock laughs
the sea laughs. The Island laughs.
The Absurd laughs.

Dearest dealer,
I with my royal straight flush,
love you so for your wild card,
that untamable, eternal, gut-driven *ha-ha*
and lucky love.

Posthumously Published Work

from *45 Mercy Street*

(1976)

Cigarettes and Whiskey and Wild, Wild Women

(from a song)

Perhaps I was born kneeling,
born coughing on the long winter,
born expecting the kiss of mercy,
born with a passion for quickness
and yet, as things progressed,
I learned early about the stockade
or taken out, the fume of the enema.
By two or three I learned not to kneel,
not to expect, to plant my fires underground
where none but the dolls, perfect and awful,
could be whispered to or laid down to die.

Now that I have written many words,
and let out so many loves, for so many,
and been altogether what I always was –
a woman of excess, of zeal and greed,
I find the effort useless.
Do I not look in the mirror,
these days,
and see a drunken rat avert her eyes?
Do I not feel the hunger so acutely
that I would rather die than look
into its face?

I kneel once more,
in case mercy should come
in the nick of time.

Food

I want mother's milk,
that good sour soup.
I want breasts singing like eggplants,
and a mouth above making kisses.
I want nipples like shy strawberries
for I need to suck the sky.
I need to bite also
as in a carrot stick.
I need arms that rock,
two clean clam shells singing *ocean*.
Further I need weeds to eat
for they are the spinach of the soul.
I am hungry and you give me
a dictionary to decipher.
I am a baby all wrapped up in its red howl
and you pour salt into my mouth.
Your nipples are stitched up like sutures
and although I suck
I suck air
and even the big fat sugar moves away.
Tell me! Tell me! Why is it?
I need food
and you walk away reading the paper.

The Money Swing

After 'Babylon Revisited' by F. Scott Fitzgerald

Mother, Father,
I hold this snapshot of you,
taken, it says, in 1929
on the deck of the yawl.
Mother, Father,
so young, so hot, so jazzy,
so like Zelda and Scott
with drinks and cigarettes and turbans
and designer slacks and frizzy permanents
and all that dough,
what do you say to me now,
here at my sweaty desk in 1971?

I know the ice in your drink is senile.
I know your smile will develop a boil.
You know only that you are on top,
swinging like children on the money swing
up and over, up and over,
until even New York City lies down small.
You know that when winter comes
and the snow comes
that it won't be real snow.
If you don't want it to be snow
you just pay money.

from Bestiary U.S.A.

Hornet

A red-hot needle
hangs out of him, he steers by it
as if it were a rudder, he
would get in the house any way he could
and then he would bounce from window
to ceiling, buzzing and looking for you.
Do not sleep for he is there wrapped in the curtain.
Do not sleep for he is there under the shelf.
Do not sleep for he wants to sew up your skin,
he wants to leap into your body like a hammer
with a nail, do not sleep he wants to get into
your nose and make a transplant, he wants do not
sleep he wants to bury your fur and make
a nest of knives, he wants to slide under your
fingernail and push in a splinter, do not sleep
he wants to climb out of the toilet when you sit on it
and make a home in the embarrassed hair do not sleep
he wants you to walk into him as into a dark fire.

Where It was At Back Then

Husband,
last night I dreamt
they cut off your hands and feet.
Husband,
you whispered to me,
Now we are both incomplete.

Husband,
I held all four
in my arms like sons and daughters.
Husband,
I bent slowly down
and washed them in magical waters.

Husband,
I placed each one
where it belonged on you.
'A miracle,'
you said and we laughed
the laugh of the well-to-do.

The Risk

When a daughter tries suicide
and the chimney falls down like a drunk
and the dog chews her tail off
and the kitchen blows up its shiny kettle
and the vacuum cleaner swallows its bag
and the toilet washes itself in tears
and the bathroom scales weigh in the ghost
of the grandmother and the windows,
those sky pieces, ride out like boats
and the grass rolls down the driveway
and the mother lies down on her marriage bed
and eats up her heart like two eggs.

45 Mercy Street

In my dream,
drilling into the marrow
of my entire bone,
my real dream,
I'm walking up and down Beacon Hill
searching for a street sign –
namely MERCY STREET.
Not there.

I try the Back Bay.
Not there.
Not there.
And yet I know the number.
45 Mercy Street.
I know the stained-glass window
of the foyer,
the three flights of the house
with its parquet floors.
I know the furniture and
mother, grandmother, great-grandmother,
the servants.
I know the cupboard of Spode,
the boat of ice, solid silver,
where the butter sits in neat squares
like strange giant's teeth
on the big mahogany table.
I know it well.
Not there.

Where did you go?
45 Mercy Street,
with great-grandmother
kneeling in her whale-bone corset
and praying gently but fiercely
to the wash basin,
at five A.M.
at noon
dozing in her wiggy rocker,
grandfather taking a nip in the pantry,
grandmother pushing the bell for the downstairs maid,
and Nana rocking Mother with an oversized flower
on her forehead to cover the curl
of when she was good and when she was . . .
And where she was begat
and in a generation
the third she will beget,
me,
with the stranger's seed blooming
into the flower called *Horrid.*

I walk in a yellow dress
and a white pocketbook stuffed with cigarettes,
enough pills, my wallet, my keys,
and being twenty-eight, or is it forty-five?
I walk. I walk.
I hold matches at the street signs
for it is dark,
as dark as the leathery dead
and I have lost my green Ford,
my house in the suburbs,
two little kids
sucked up like pollen by the bee in me
and a husband
who has wiped off his eyes
in order not to see my inside out

and I am walking and looking
and this is no dream
just my oily life
where the people are alibis
and the street is unfindable for an
entire lifetime.

Pull the shades down –
I don't care!
Bolt the door, mercy,
erase the number,
rip down my street sign,
what can it matter,
what can it matter to this cheapskate
who wants to own the past
that went out on a dead ship
and left me only with paper?

Not there.

I open my pocketbook,
as women do,
and fish swim back and forth
between the dollars and the lipstick.
I pick them out,
one by one
and throw them at the street signs,
and shoot my pocketbook
into the Charles River.
Next I pull the dream off
and slam into the cement wall
of the clumsy calendar
I live in,
my life,
and its hauled up
notebooks.

from *Words for Dr. Y.*

(1978)

from Letters to Dr. Y.

(1960-1970)

Dr. Y.
I need a thin hot wire,
your Rescue Inc. voice
to stretch me out,
to keep me from going underfoot
and growing stiff
as a yardstick.

Death,
I need your hot breath,
my index finger in the flame,
two cretins standing at my ears,
listening for the cop car.

Death,
I need a little cradle
to carry me out,
a boxcar for my books,
a nickel in my palm,
and no kiss
on my kiss.

Death,
I need my little addiction to you.
I need that tiny voice who,
even as I rise from the sea,
all woman, all there,
says kill me, kill me.

My manic eye
sees only the trapeze artist
who flies without a net.
Bravo, I cry,
swallowing the pills,
the do die pills.
Listen ducky,
death is as close to pleasure
as a toothpick.
To die whole,
riddled with nothing
but desire for it,
is like breakfast
after love.

February 16, 1960

What has it come to, Dr. Y.
my needing you?
I work days,
stuffed into a pine-paneled box.
You work days
with your air conditioner gasping
like a tube-fed woman.
I move my thin legs into your office
and we work over the cadaver of my soul.
We make a stage set out of my past
and stuff painted puppets into it.
We make a bridge toward my future
and I cry to you: I will be steel!
I will build a steel bridge over my need!
I will build a bomb shelter over my heart!
But my future is a secret.
It is as shy as a mole.

What has it come to
my needing you . . .
I am the irritating pearl
and you are the necessary shell.
You are the twelve faces of the Atlantic
and I am the rowboat. I am the burden.

How dependent, the fox asks?
Why so needy, the snake sings?
It's this way . . .
Time after time I fall down into the well
and you dig a tunnel in the dangerous sand,

you take the altar from a church and shore it up.
With your own white hands you dig me out.
You give me hoses so I can breathe.
You make me a skull to hold the worms
of my brains. You give me hot chocolate
although I am known to have no belly.
The trees are whores yet you place
me under them. The sun is poison
yet you toss me under it like a rose.
I am out of practice at living.
You are as brave as a motorcycle.

What has it come to
that I should defy you?
I would be a copper wire
without electricity.
I would be a Beacon Hill dowager
without her hat.
I would be a surgeon
who cut with his own nails.
I would be a glutton
who threw away his spoon.
I would be God
without Jesus to speak for me.

I would be Jesus
without a cross to prove me.

August 24, 1964

I called him *Comfort*.
Dr. Y., I gave him the wrong name.
I should have called him *Preacher*
for all day there on the coastland
he read me the Bible.
He read me the Bible to prove I was sinful.
For in the night he was betrayed.
And then he let me give him a Judas-kiss,
that red lock that held us in place,
and then I gave him a drink from my cup
and he whispered, 'Rape, rape.'
And then I gave him my wrist
and he sucked on the blood,
hating himself for it,
murmuring, 'God will see. God will see.'

And I said,
'To hell with God!'

And he said,
'Would you mock God?'

And I said,
'God is only mocked by believers!'

And he said,
'I love only the truth.'

And I said,
'This holy concern for the truth –
no one worries about it except liars.'

And God was bored.
He turned on his side
like an opium eater
and slept.

March 28, 1965

I'm dreaming the My Lai soldier again,
I'm dreaming the My Lai soldier night after night.
He rings the doorbell like the Fuller Brush Man
and wants to shake hands with me
and I do because it would be rude to say no
and I look at my hand and it is green
with intestines.
And they won't come off,
they won't. He apologizes for this over and over.
The My Lai soldier lifts me up again and again
and lowers me down with the other dead women and babies
saying, *It's my job. It's my job.*

Then he gives me a bullet to swallow
like a sleeping tablet.
I am lying in this belly of dead babies
each one belching up the yellow gasses of death
and their mothers tumble, eyeballs, knees, upon me,
each for the last time, each authentically dead.
The soldier stands on a stepladder above us
pointing his red penis right at me and saying,
Don't take this personally.

December 17, 1969

from *Last Poems*

Admonitions to a Special Person

Watch out for power,
for its avalanche can bury you,
snow, snow, snow, smothering your mountain.

Watch out for hate,
it can open its mouth and you'll fling yourself out
to eat off your leg, an instant leper.

Watch out for friends,
because when you betray them,
as you will,
they will bury their heads in the toilet
and flush themselves away.

Watch out for intellect,
because it knows so much it knows nothing
and leaves you hanging upside down,
mouthing knowledge as your heart
falls out of your mouth.

Watch out for games, the actor's part,
the speech planned, known, given,
for they will give you away
and you will stand like a naked little boy,
pissing on your own child-bed.

Watch out for love
(unless it is true,
and every part of you says yes including the toes),

it will wrap you up like a mummy,
and your scream won't be heard
and none of your running will run.

Love? Be it man. Be it woman.
It must be a wave you want to glide in on,
give your body to it, give your laugh to it,
give, when the gravelly sand takes you,
your tears to the land. To love another is something
like prayer and can't be planned, you just fall
into its arms because your belief undoes your disbelief.

Special person,
if I were you I'd pay no attention
to admonitions from me,
made somewhat out of your words
and somewhat out of mine.
A collaboration.
I do not believe a word I have said,
except some, except I think of you like a young tree
with pasted-on leaves and know you'll root
and the real green thing will come.

Let go. Let go.
Oh special person,
possible leaves,
this typewriter likes you on the way to them,
but wants to break crystal glasses
in celebration,
for you,
when the dark crust is thrown off
and you float all around
like a happened balloon.

As It was Written

Earth, earth,
riding your merry-go-round
toward extinction,
right to the roots,
thickening the oceans like gravy,
festering in your caves,
you are becoming a latrine.
Your trees are twisted chairs.
Your flowers moan at their mirrors,
and cry for a sun that doesn't wear a mask.

Your clouds wear white,
trying to become nuns
and say novenas to the sky.
The sky is yellow with its jaundice,
and its veins spill into the rivers
where the fish kneel down
to swallow hair and goat's eyes.

All in all, I'd say,
the world is strangling.
And I, in my bed each night,
listen to my twenty shoes
converse about it.
And the moon,
under its dark hood,
falls out of the sky each night,
with its hungry red mouth
to suck at my scars.

Love Letter Written in a Burning Building

Dearest Foxxy,

I am in a crate,
the crate that was ours,
full of white shirts and salad greens,
the icebox knocking at our delectable knocks,
and I wore movies in my eyes,
and you wore eggs in your tunnel,
and we played sheets, sheets, sheets
all day, even in the bathtub like lunatics.
But today I set the bed a fire
and smoke is filling the room,
it is getting hot enough for the walls to melt,
and the icebox, a gluey white tooth.

I have on a mask in order to write my last words,
and they are just for you, and I will place them
in the icebox saved for vodka and tomatoes,
and perhaps they will last.
The dog will not. Her spots will fall off.
The old letters will melt into a black bee.
The nightgowns are already shredding
into paper, the yellow, the red, the purple.
The bed – well, the sheets have turned to gold –
hard, hard gold, and the mattress
is being kissed into a stone.

As for me, my dearest Foxxy,
my poems to you may or may not reach the icebox
and its hopeful eternity,

for isn't yours enough?
The one where you name
my name right out in P. R.?
If my toes weren't yielding to pitch
I'd tell the whole story –
not just the sheet story
but the belly-button story,
the pried-eyelid story,
the whiskey-sour-of-the-nipple story –
and shovel back our love where it belonged.

Despite my asbestos gloves,
the cough is filling me with black,
and a red powder seeps through my veins,
our little crate goes down so publicly
and without meaning it, you see,
meaning a solo act,
a cremation of the love,
but instead we seem to be going down
right in the middle of a Russian street,
the flames making the sound of
the horse being beaten and beaten,
the whip is adoring its human triumph
while the flies wait, blow by blow,
straight from United Fruit, Inc.

In Excelsis

It is half winter, half spring,
and Barbara and I are standing
confronting the ocean.
Its mouth is open very wide,
and it has dug up its green,
throwing it, throwing it at the shore.
You say it is angry.
I say it is like a kicked Madonna.
Its womb collapses, drunk with its fever.
We breathe in its fury.

I, the inlander,
am here with you for just a small space.
I am almost afraid,
so long gone from the sea.
I have seen her smooth as a cheek.
I have seen her easy,
doing her business,
lapping in.
I have seen her rolling her hoops of blue.
I have seen her tear the land off.
I have seen her drown me twice,
and yet not take me.
You tell me that as the green drains backward
it covers Britain,
but have you never stood on *that* shore
and seen it cover you?

We have come to worship,
the tongues of the surf are prayers,
and we vow,
the unspeakable vow.
Both silently.
Both differently.
I wish to enter her like a dream,
leaving my roots here on the beach
like a pan of knives.
And my past to unravel, with its knots and snarls,
and walk into ocean,
letting it explode over me
and outward, where I would drink the moon
and my clothes would slip away,
and I would sink into the great mother arms
I never had,
except here where the abyss
throws itself on the sand
blow by blow,
over and over,
and we stand on the shore
loving its pulse
as it swallows the stars,
and has since it all began
and will continue into oblivion,
past our knowing
and the wild toppling green that enters us today,
for a small time
in half winter, half spring.

April 1, 1974

THE FEMININE MYSTIQUE

Betty Friedan

When Betty Friedan produced *The Feminine Mystique* in 1963, she could not have realized how the discovery and debate of her contemporaries' general malaise would shake up society. Victims of a false belief system, these women were following strict social convention by loyally conforming to the pretty image of the magazines, and found themselves forced to seek meaning in their lives only through a family and a home. Friedan's controversial book about these women – and every woman – would ultimately set Second Wave feminism in motion and begin the battle for equality.

This groundbreaking and life-changing work remains just as powerful, important and true as it was forty-five years ago, and is essential reading both as a historical document and as a study of women living in a man's world.

'One of the most influential nonfiction books of the twentieth century' *The New York Times*

LITTLE BIRDS

Anaïs Nin

Delta of Venus and *Little Birds*, Anaïs Nin's bestselling volumes of erotica, contain striking revelations of a woman's sexuality and inner life. In *Little Birds*, each of the thirteen short stories captures a moment of sexual awakening, recognition or fulfilment, and reveals the subtle or explicit means by which men and women are aroused. Lust, obsession, fantasy and desire emerge as part of the human condition, as pure or as complex as any other of its aspects.

'One of the most extraordinary and unconventional writers of this century' *The New York Times Book Review*

MY POEMS WON'T CHANGE THE WORLD

Patrizia Cavalli

Two hours ago I fell in love
and trembled, and tremble still,
and haven't a clue whom I should tell.

Any hall she reads her poetry in is invariably filled to the gills. In Italy, Patrizia Cavalli is as beloved as Wisława Szymborska is in Poland, and if Italy were Japan she'd be designated a national treasure. The Italian philosopher Giorgio Agamben said of Cavalli that she has written 'the most intensely ethical poetry in Italian literature of the 20th century'. One could add that it is, easily, also the most sensual and comical. Though Cavalli has been widely translated into German, French and Spanish, she remains too little known in Britain; *My Poems Won't Change the World* is the first substantial gathering of translations of her work into the English language.

The book is made up of poems from Cavalli's collections published by Einaudi from 1974 to 2006, here translated by an illustrious group of poets including Mark Strand, Jorie Graham, Jonathan Galassi and Gini Alhadeff. Thoughtful, sly and full of life, these are poems of the self, the body, pasta, cats, the city traversed on foot or by car, and – always, and above all – love.

SELECTED POEMS

Federico García Lorca

Spain's greatest and most well-loved modern poet, Lorca has long been admired for the emotional intensity and dark brilliance of his work, which drew on music, drama, mythology and the songs of his Andalucian childhood. From the playful *Suites* and stylized *Gypsy Ballads*, to his own dark vision of urban life, *Poet in New York*, and his elegiac meditation on death, *Lament for Ignacio Sánchez Mejías*, his range was remarkable. This bilingual edition provides versions by distinguished poets and translators, drawing on every book of poems published by Lorca and on his uncollected works.

'His poems are uniquely compelling and accessible . . . he had *duende* . . . a sort of spirit-possession, an unearthly artistic energy' *The Times*